ANCIENT HISTORY

Workbook

ANCIENT HISTORY

Workbook

Hanael Bianchi

TAN Books
Gastonia, North Carolina

Compiled by Hanael Bianchi

Cover design by Caroline Green

Cover image: The Parthenon at Athens (engraving), Bartlett, William Henry (1809-54), © Look and Learn / Bridgeman Images

ISBN: 978-1-5051-2187-2

Published in the United States by
TAN Books
PO Box 269
Gastonia, NC 28053
www.TANBooks.com
Printed in the United States of America

Contents

Introduction

This guidebook provides prompts for weekly vocabulary assignments, quizzes, writing assignments, and outlines. They can be found in the weekly lessons. The course lesson plan has a schedule with suggested due dates for these assignments. Weeks 15 and 30 are reserved for the midterm and final. The guidebook contains a study guide for the exams, instructions on how to construct the exams, and sample exams. The following pages of the introduction provide detailed instructions for each type of assignment, sample assignments, grading guidelines, and grading rubrics.

Vocabulary Assignments

Instructions

Every lesson has three vocabulary terms, which are key individuals, events, or concepts from the lesson. Students should review the terms before reading the textbook and watching the lecture video, and when completing these learning activities, they should take thorough notes when the terms are reviewed. These notes will help students construct the vocabulary identifications.

Each identification should be five sentences long and answer what/who, when, where, and why. The "what/who" is a one-sentence summary of key information, like a definition. The "when" is the dates associated with the term, which should be precise for a person or event but a general period for a concept. The "where" is the location. The "why" is a three-sentence summary of why the term is important, and it should highlight the most significant historical points.

Sample "Exceeds" for Napoleon

What/who: Napoleon was a French military leader who became emperor of France.
When and Where: He was born in Corsica in 1769, reigned as emperor of France from 1804–1814, 1815, and died in exile in 1821.

Why: He was one of the greatest military leaders in history, conquered most of continental Europe, and defeated numerous coalitions. In his conquests, he spread the ideology of the French Revolution, challenged feudalism, and enacted a new legal system, helping to create the modern, secular state. He overextended his empire during his failed invasion of Russia, and he was finally defeated at Waterloo in 1815, leading to a permanent exile.

Sample "Meets" for Napoleon

What/who: Napoleon was a great military leader in France.

When and Where: He lived 1769–1821, mainly in France

Why: He conquered most of continental Europe and defeated numerous coalitions. He spread modern ideology and enacted a new legal system to create the modern, secular state. He failed in his invasion of Russia and was defeated at Waterloo.

Grading

Each vocabulary term is worth 5 points. The what/who, when, and where are each worth 1 point, and the why is worth 3 points.

Rubric

	Exceeds	Meets	Does Not Meet	Fails
What/Who	1 Point Constructs a concise and clear definition with connections to specific historical information.	.8 Points Constructs a concise and clear definition without connections to specific historical information.	.6 Points Constructs a concise definition but contains inaccurate information.	.4–0 Points Constructs a definition that is not clear and contains mostly inaccurate information.
When and Where	1 Point Accurately identifies when and where with historical details.	.8 Points Accurately identifies when and where without details.	.6 Points Partially identifies where and when accurately.	.4–0 Points Inaccurately identifies where and when.
Why	3 Points Highlights the most significant information and provides several historical details in every sentence.	2.4 Points Highlights significant information but does not provide several historical details in every sentence.	.18 Points Highlights historical information that is not significant and does not provide historical details.	.12–0 Points Inaccurately highlights historical information that is not significant.

Quizzes

Instructions

After completing the textbook reading and lecture videos, students will complete a ten-question quiz, which is contained in the weekly lesson. Students should be allotted a finite amount of time (ten minutes is suggested) to complete the quiz. They can use their notes and textbook while taking the quiz, but they should not have access to the internet. The intent of the quiz is not to force students to memorize the content but to check that they have watched the video and read the textbook.

Grading

After completing the quiz, students can check their answers using the answer key at the end of the guidebook. The quiz is worth 10 points, with each question worth 1 point. The answer key also has the page numbers of the answers from the textbook.

Writing Assignments

Instructions

Students are asked to read a primary source located in the weekly lessons. They will then write a short response paper based on a question(s) about the source and related to the theme of the lesson. The historical documents assigned in the guidebook were written during a different time and culture, and they might be difficult to comprehend after the first read. The response paper will build on background information in the textbook and lecture, but students might still have to read the documents several times and research difficult words or concepts. Composing the response paper will require analysis and critical thinking skills.

Before writing the paper, students should construct an outline. The first step is to develop a one-sentence answer to the question(s), and this sentence is the thesis. Next, they should find several (2 to 3) quotes from the primary source that supports the thesis. Lastly, they need to compose topic sentences that connect the thesis and quotes. It will be helpful with the grading process to clearly mark the thesis and topic sentences (underline) and to place the quotes in quotation marks followed by the document name in paratheses.

Once the outline is complete, students can begin writing the paper. The first paragraph should be a short introduction that provides context and contains the thesis. The introduction is followed by several body paragraphs (2 to 3) that begin with a topic sentence and have direct quotes as evidence. The paper ends with a short conclusion.

Sample Writing Assignment

Prompt: Read the following excerpt from the *Ashley Mines Commission*. Write a short 300-word essay answering the following questions: What were the working conditions for child laborers during the Industrial Revolution? Why should child labor have been outlawed?

The Industrial Revolution resulted in rapid urbanization as laborers flocked to cities looking for jobs in factories. Many factories turned to child labor to cut costs, but this created many problems. Child labor should have been outlawed because of the horrible conditions and lack of education.

(The introduction provides the context of the Industrial Revolution, and the thesis, which is underlined, answers the assigned questions.)

The conditions associated with child labor were inhumane and damaged the health of those involved. Children were required to work long hours doing difficult tasks, and they were under the constant threat of punishment. Isabella Read, 12 years old, worked as a coal-bearer. She recounted, "I make from pit's bottom to wall face and back, thinks about 30 or 25 on the average; the distance varies from 100 to 250 fathom. I carry about 1 cwt. and a quarter on my back; have to stoop much and creep through water, which is frequently up to the calves of my leg" (Ashley Mines Commission). She also complained about the high temperatures, trouble breathing, and that the lights would often be turned off. Considering the health risks, this was not a safe environment for children to be spending their days.

Child laborers during the Industrial Revolution also received very little education. Some children would only attend Sunday school, while others had no education. Mary Barrett, aged 14, stated that only one of her twelve brothers and sisters could read and none of them could write. She said, "They never went to day-school, but three of them go to Sunday-school" (Ashley Mines Commission). This lack of education created an entire generation that was ignorant of the truth and harmed their future as well as the future of the country.

(The two body paragraphs provide evidence to support the argument outlined in the thesis. Note that the topic sentences, which are underlined, connect the quotes to the thesis. The quotes provide evidence, and they should be around 25 percent of the text, not more.)

Child laborers had to work in horrible conditions and received little to no education. This evil institution caused long-lasting physical and mental problems, and thus, it should have been outlawed for children to work in this environment.

(The short conclusion reiterates the argument found in the thesis. The word count is 309, which surpasses the 300-word minimum. There is no maximum word count.)

Grading

The response paper is worth 25 points. It is graded on the argument, which is worth 10 points, and structure, use of document(s), and mechanics, each worth 5 points.

Rubric

	Exceeds	Meets	Does Not Meet	Fails
Argument	10 Points The thesis and topic sentences are easily identifiable, crystal clear, and insightfully answer the question(s).	8 Points The thesis and topic sentences are easily identifiable and slightly unclear or lack insight in answering the question(s).	6 Points The thesis and topic sentences are not easily identifiable, are unclear, and lack insight when answering the question(s).	4–0 Points Has no identifiable or utterly incompetent thesis and topic sentences.
Structure	5 Points The introduction and conclusion clearly summarize the argument, body paragraphs support the topic sentences, and paragraphs have seamless transitions.	4 Points The introduction and conclusion summarize the argument, body paragraphs wander from the topic sentences, and paragraphs have a few awkward transitions.	3 Points The introduction and conclusion do not summarize the argument, body paragraphs are unclear or jump around, and paragraphs have mostly awkward transitions.	2–0 Points The paper does not have separate paragraphs and jumps from point to point with awkward transitions

	Exceeds	Meets	Does Not Meet	Fails
Use of Document(s)	5 Points One direct quote to support every topic sentence with excellent integration. Factual information is incorporated.	4 Points One direct quote to support every topic sentence with good integration. Some factual information is incorporated.	3 Points One direct quote to support every topic sentence with poor integration. Limited factual information is incorporated.	2–0 Points Topic sentences are not supported by a direct quote. Factual information is not incorporated.
Mechanics	5 Points Language is clear. Correct word usage, punctuation, sentence structure, and grammar. No spelling errors or run-on sentences. Exceeds the 300-word minimum.	4 Points Sentence structure and grammar has occasional lapse. Some spelling errors and at least one run-on sentence or sentence fragment. Exceeds the 300-word minimum.	3 Points Problems in sentence structure and grammar. Multiple errors in punctuation and spelling. Several run-on sentences and sentence fragments. Does not meet the 300-word minimum.	2–0 Points Huge problems in sentence structure and grammar. Frequent errors in punctuation and spelling. May have many run-on sentences and sentence fragments. Does not meet the 300-word minimum.

Outline

Instructions

At the end of each weekly lesson, students are asked to create an outline based on a question(s). The material for the outline should come from all the activities completed throughout the week. As with the response paper, the outline should have a thesis and topic sentences. Instead of direct quotes, there should be several (3 to 5) sentences to support each topic sentence.

Sample Outline

Prompt: How was World War I fought? How did the war impact politics and the individuals who fought in it?

- Thesis: World War I was fought in a radically new fashion based on new weapons, and it had a great impact on the politics and individuals of the period.
    - a. Topic Sentence 1: World War I was fought using trench warfare and several new weapons were introduced.
        - i. On the Western Front, the war was fought using trenches on opposing sides and with an unoccupied area between them.
        - ii. The advantage was to the defender in this system, and offensive assaults were largely ineffective, such as the battles of Somme and Verdun.
        - iii. Modern weapons like machine guns, advanced artillery, and chemical weapons increased the destructive nature of the war.
        - iv. Tanks and airplanes were introduced, but they were not effectively used to break the stalemate.
    - b. The political landscape in Europe and beyond changed dramatically due to the war.
        - i. Before the war, most of the great powers were ruled by monarchs and connected through a system of alliances.
        - ii. Due to the war, the multiethnic Ottoman and Austrian empires were divided into numerous small states.
        - iii. The Russian Tsar was removed and killed, and a communist state under Lenin came into existence.
        - iv. Germany became a republic, faced harsh punishment, and blamed for the war.
        - v. The League of Nations was formed to prevent future wars but was a weak institution and destined to fail.
    - c. The war had a profound effect on the individuals who fought in it and their community.
        - i. World War I resulted in 20 million deaths and 21 million wounded.
        - ii. Survivors experience severe trauma, then labeled shell shock (now PTSD), and had difficulty returning to normal life.
        - iii. Women played a large role on the home front, and thus, several countries extended the vote to females after the war.
        - iv. After the war, traditional values were discarded by many, resulting in the liberal 1920s.

Grading

The outlines are worth 10 points with organization and content both worth 5 points each.

Rubric

	Exceeds	Meets	Does Not Meet	Fails
Organization	5 Points The thesis, topic sentences, and evidence clearly and logically support each other. Several sentences support each topic sentence.	4 Points The thesis, topic sentences, and evidence partially support each other. Several sentences support each topic sentence.	3 Points The thesis, topic sentences, and evidence do not support each other. One or two sentences support each topic sentence.	2–0 Points There is not a distinguishable thesis and topic sentences. Topic sentences are not supported with evidence.
Content	5 Points The outline contains accurate information and numerous historical facts.	4 Points The outline contains mostly accurate information and numerous historical facts.	3 Points The outline contains some accurate information and a few historical facts.	2–0 Points The outline contains mostly inaccurate information and a few historical facts.

Exams

Instructions and sample exams are contained in lessons 15 and 30.

Calculating a Final Course Grade

- ☐ 28 Quizzes x 10 points = 280
- ☐ 84 Vocabulary Assignments x 5 points = 420
- ☐ 28 Response Papers x 25 points = 700
- ☐ 28 Outlines x 10 points = 280
- ☐ 2 Exams x 200 points = 400
- ☐ Total Points = 2080

Students can use the following sheet to record grades. At the end of the course, the total points earned can be divided by the total points available to calculate a percentage grade.

Week	Quiz	Vocab	Paper	Outline	Exam
1					x
2					x
3					x
4					x
5					x
6					x
7					x
8					x
9					x
10					x
11					x
12					x
13					x
14					x
15	x	x	x	x	
16					x
17					x
18					x
19					x
20					x
21					x
22					x
23					x
24					x
25					x
26					x
27					x
28					x
29					x
30	x	x	x	x	
Total					

Lesson 1

Introduction

Vocabulary

Define each term in 5 sentences.

Ancient History

Christendom

Western Civilization

Quiz

From the Lecture

1. One of the course objectives is to discover the connection between Ancient History and your life.
    A. True
    B. False

2. Warren Carroll founded what college?
    A. Franciscan University
    B. Christendom College
    C. Magdalen College
    D. St. Thomas Aquinas College

3. History is _______ for inquiry or knowledge that results from inquiry.
    A. Latin
    B. German
    C. Greek
    D. Hebrew

4. What source provides the best evidence to answer a historical question?
    A. History Teacher
    B. Textbook
    C. Primary Source
    D. Secondary Source

5. The academic discipline of ancient history begins with:
    A. creation.
    B. farming.
    C. written documents.
    D. the birth of Jesus.

6. "Civilization" is based on the Latin word for farming.
    A. True
    B. False

7. What other civilization is as ancient as Western Civilization?
    A. Indo-European
    B. Mayan
    C. Russian
    D. Chinese

From the Textbook

8. Christendom is the reign of God recognized by men.
    A. True
    B. False

9. The history of Christendom is different from the history of Christianity due to:
    A. emphasis on different time periods.
    B. a more thematic approach.
    C. greater focus on the laity and temporal affairs.

10. Historical objectivity requires:
    A. honesty and respect for truth.
    B. having no point of view.
    C. ignoring opposing views.

Writing Assignment

Read the following excerpt from St. Augustine's *The City of God*. Write a short 300-word essay answering the following questions. What are the characteristics of the two cities? What is St. Augustine's view of history and how does it relate to the idea of Christendom?

The City of God, Volume II

Book 14: 1. That the disobedience of the first man would have plunged all men into the endless misery of the second death, had not the grace of God rescued many.

We have already stated in the preceding books that God, desiring not only that the human race might be able by their similarity of nature to associate with one another, but also that they might be bound together in harmony and peace by the ties of relationship, was pleased to derive all men from one individual, and created man with such a nature that the members of the race should not have died, had not the two first (of whom the one was created out of nothing, and the other out of him) merited this by their disobedience; for by them so great a sin was committed, that by it the human nature was altered for the worse, and was transmitted also to their posterity, liable to sin and subject to death. And the kingdom of death so reigned over men, that the deserved penalty of sin would have hurled all headlong even into the second death, of which there is no end, had not the undeserved grace of God saved some therefrom. And thus it has come to pass, that though there are very many and great nations all over the earth, whose rites and customs, speech, arms, and dress, are distinguished by marked differences, yet there are no more than two kinds of human society, which we may justly call two cities, according to the language of our Scriptures. The one consists of those who wish to live after the flesh, the other of those who wish to live after the spirit; and when they severally achieve what they wish, they live in peace, each after their kind.

Book 14: 28. Of the nature of the two cities, the earthly and the heavenly.

Accordingly, two cities have been formed by two loves: the earthly by the love of self, even to the contempt of God; the heavenly by the love of God, even to the contempt of self. The former, in a word, glories in itself, the latter in the Lord. For the one seeks glory from men; but the greatest glory of the other is God, the witness of conscience. The one lifts up its head in its own glory; the other says to its God, "Thou art my glory, and the lifter up of mine head." In the one, the princes and the nations it subdues are ruled by the love of ruling; in the other, the princes and the subjects serve one another in love, the latter obeying, while the former take thought for all. The one delights in its own strength, represented in the persons of its rulers; the other says to its God, "I will love Thee, O Lord, my strength." And therefore the wise men of the one city, living according to man, have sought for profit to their own bodies or souls, or both, and those who have known God "glorified Him not as God, neither were thankful, but became vain in their imaginations, and their foolish heart was darkened; professing themselves to be wise,"—that is, glorying in their own wisdom, and being possessed by pride,—"they became fools, and changed the glory of the incorruptible God into an image made like to corruptible man, and to birds, and four-footed beasts, and creeping things." For they were either leaders or followers of the people in adoring images, "and worshipped and served the creature more than the Creator, who is blessed for ever." But in the other city there is no human wisdom, but only godliness, which offers due worship to the true God, and looks for its reward in the society of the saints, of holy angels as well as holy men, "that God may be all in all."[1]

---

1 Aurelius Augustine. *The City of God, Volume II*, eBook. Edited by Marcus Dodds. Gutenberg Project. http://www.gutenberg.org/files/45305/45305-h/45305-h.htm#Page_1. Accessed February 6, 2021.

Outline

Construct an outline for an essay on the following questions. What is history? How are ancient history, Christendom, and Western Civilization similar and different?

Lesson 2

Ancient Mesopotamia

Vocabulary

Define each term in 5 sentences.

Agricultural (Neolithic) Revolution

Characteristics of a Civilization

Ancient Mesopotamia

Quiz

From the Lecture

1. What enabled the creation of civilizations?
   - A. stone tools
   - B. farming
   - C. bronze
   - D. writing

2. Which one of the following is NOT an early farming settlement?
   - A. Catal Huyuk
   - B. Jerusalem
   - C. Jericho

3. What was the first civilization to expand trade with ships and the wheel?
   - A. Sumerians
   - B. Egyptians
   - C. Babylonians
   - D. Persians

4. Early cuneiform was written on:
   - A. paper.
   - B. palm leaves.
   - C. clay.
   - D. animal skin.

5. Ur, Uruk, and Lagash are cities of what civilization?
   - A. Egypt
   - B. Sumer
   - C. Palestine

6. "Mesopotamia" means the land between two rivers.
   - A. True
   - B. False

7. Bronze is made from copper and nickel.
   - A. True
   - B. False

From the Textbook

8. All the following are characteristics of an ancient city EXCEPT:
   - A. shrines.
   - B. walls.
   - C. markets.
   - D. baths.

9. The ancient moat surrounding Jericho was:
   - A. 20 ft wide and 6 ft deep.
   - B. 27 ft wide and 9 ft deep.
   - C. 10 ft wide and 4 ft deep.

10. The oldest epic tells the story of:
    - A. Sargon.
    - B. Melchizedek.
    - C. Moses.
    - D. Gilgamesh.

Writing Assignment

Read the following excerpt from the *Epic of Gilgamesh*. Write a short 300-word essay answering the following questions. How does Gilgamesh mourn Enkidu's death and what was his view of death? How do you think death impacted religion in the ancient world?

The Epic of Gilgamesh Tablets 8 and 9

There is none other tree like unto thee;
Six gar [1 gar = 12 or 14 cubits] *is* thy height and two gar thy thickness.

Enkidu also says of it, "I know thee."

"In good health I went forth, my friend. * * *
But the dream which I dreamed has been fulfilled."
And there lay Enkidu for twelve days [on the first and the second day?]
on which Enkidu on his couch [lay sick?];
On the third and the fourth * * *;
On the fifth, sixth, seventh, eighth, etc., day
on which Enkidu [lay sick on his couch?]
The eleventh, the twelfth day * * *
On which Enkidu lay on his couch * * *
Then he called to Gilgamesh.
Gilgamesh wept bitterly over the loss of his friend
Enkidu, and he lay stretched out upon the ground, (saying):
"I will not die like Enkidu,
But weeping has entered into my heart;
Fear of death has befallen me, and
I lie here stretched out upon the ground.
To (test) the strength of Utnapishtim, the son of Kidin-Marduk,
I will set out, and I will go at once."
"At the mountain ravine I arrived by night-time,
* * * Lions I saw, and I was afraid;
* * * but I lifted my head to god Sin and I prayed.
To the [great?] majesty of the god came my cry,
[and he hearkened] and saved me, even me."
And in the night he saw?] a vision and a dream,
Lions * * *] were enjoying themselves."
And he lifted the axe in his hand,
and drew out the sword from his belt.
Like a javelin he threw himself between them;
he wounded, killed, and scattered [them?]

[The rest of the column is lost.]

of a mountain whose name is Mashu.
As he came to the mountain of Mashu,
whose entrance is guarded daily by monsters,
whose back extends to the dam of heaven,
and whose breast reaches down to Aralu,

Scorpion-men guard its gate;
Dreadful terror they spread, and it is death to behold them.
Their splendour is fearful, overthrowing the mountains;
From sunrise to sunset they guard the sun.
Gilgamesh beheld them, and with fear
and terror his face grew dark.
His mind became confused at the wildness of their aspect.
But one scorpion-man said to his wife:
"He that there cometh to us, flesh of the gods is his body."
And the wife answered the scorpion-man:
"Two (thirds) he resembles a god, and one third only a man."
And the scorpion-man replied and said unto her:
["One] of the gods has given the order;
[and] he has travelled over far-distant roads,
until he should come unto me.
The mountains] which he has crossed are steep."

[The remainder is broken away.]

Col. III, as far as the fragments permit us to see, narrates that Gilgamesh, seeing that the monster regarded him with friendly eyes, recovered from his fright and told the scorpion-man of his intention to go "to Utnapishtim, his ancestor, who had been removed into the assembly of the gods and [had thus power over] life and death." The scorpion-man replied by describing to Gilgamesh the difficulties and dangers connected with such a march through the mountain of Mashu. Nobody has yet been able to do so, twelve miles of heavy darkness in all directions having to be penetrated. But the hero was not discouraged, and the scorpion-man acceded to his urgent request and opened to him the gate of the mountain; and now begins the wearisome march:

One mile he marches, thick is the darkness, not does it grow light.
Two miles he marches, thick is the darkness, not does it grow light.

Col. V (p. 65) continues the description of the twelve-mile walk in the same diffuse epic style; then the hero leaves the mountain and—on the shore of the sea—beholds a beautiful and wonderful tree:

And as he saw it, he ran toward it.
Diamonds (?) it bore as fruit,
Branches were hanging (down?), beautiful to behold.
Crystal (antimony?) the branches bore;
with fruit it was laden, dazzling the eye (of the hero).
Other precious trees are also there.[2]

2 *The Epic of Gligamesh*. Translated by William Muss-Arnolt (1901). Jason and the Argonauts through the Ages (website). http://www.argonauts-book.com/english-translation-of-gilgamesh.html.

Outline

Construct an outline for an essay on the following questions. What is a civilization? What are the main characteristics of Ancient Mesopotamia?

Lesson 3

Ancient Egypt and India

Vocabulary

Define each term in 5 sentences.

Nile River

Pharaoh

Indus River Valley Civilization

Quiz

From the Lecture

1. How could the floods of the Nile River best be described?
   A. violent
   B. predictable
   C. destructive
   D. mysterious

2. Egypt was considered the "breadbasket" of the ancient world.
   A. True
   B. False

3. Lower Egypt is a southern region of the country.
   A. True
   B. False

4. Who was the first king to unite Egypt?
   A. Ramses I
   B. Akhenaton
   C. Tutankhamun
   D. Narmer

5. What is NOT a period of Egyptian history?
    A. Early Kingdom
    B. First Intermediate Period
    C. Middle Kingdom
    D. Old Kingdom

6. Before the pyramids, the pharaohs were buried in flat rectangular structures called:
    A. ziggurats.
    B. bent pyramids.
    C. dolmens.
    D. mastabas.

7. Which of the following is NOT a major site of the Indus River Valley Civilization?
    A. Mohenjo-Daro
    B. Istakhr
    C. Harappa

8. What ancient books are attributed to the Indo-European invaders into Ancient India?
    A. Homeric Epics
    B. Vedas
    C. Avesta

From the Textbook

9. In Indian history, invaders conquered a people called:
    A. Brahmins.
    B. Sikhs.
    C. Jains.
    D. Dasyus.

10. Merchants from the Indus River Civilization travelled to what other ancient Civilization?
    A. Mesopotamia
    B. Egypt
    C. Greece

Writing Assignment

Read the *Hymn to the Nile*. Write a short 300-word essay answering the following questions. What was the Egyptians view of the Nile? In ancient Egypt, what was the connection between nature and religion?

Hymn to the Nile

Hail to thee, O Nile! Who manifests thyself over this land, and comes to give life to Egypt! Mysterious is thy issuing forth from the darkness, on this day whereon it is celebrated! Watering the orchards created by Re, to cause all the cattle to live, you give the earth to drink, inexhaustible one! Path that descends from the sky, loving the bread of Seb and the first-fruits of Nepera, You cause the workshops of Ptah to prosper!

Lord of the fish, during the inundation, no bird alights on the crops. You create the grain, you bring forth the barley, assuring perpetuity to the temples. If you cease your toil and your work, then all that exists is in anguish. If the gods suffer in heaven, then the faces of men waste away.

Then He torments the flocks of Egypt, and great and small are in agony. But all is changed for mankind when He comes; He is endowed with the qualities of Nun. If He shines, the earth is joyous, every stomach is full of rejoicing, every spine is happy, every jaw-bone crushes.

He brings the offerings, as chief of provisioning; He is the creator of all good things, as master of energy, full of sweetness in his choice. If offerings are made it is thanks to Him. He brings forth the herbage for the flocks, and sees that each god receives his sacrifices. All that depends on Him is a precious incense. He spreads himself over Egypt, filling the granaries, renewing the marts, watching over the goods of the unhappy.

He is prosperous to the height of all desires, without fatiguing Himself therefor. He brings again his lordly bark; He is not sculptured in stone, in the statutes crowned with the uraeus serpent, He cannot be contemplated. No servitors has He, no bearers of offerings! He is not enticed by incantations! None knows the place where He dwells, none discovers his retreat by the power of a written spell.

No dwelling which may contain you! None penetrates within your heart! Your young men, your children applaud you and render unto you royal homage. Stable are your decrees for Egypt before your servants of the North! He stanches the water from all eyes and watches over the increase of his good things.

Where misery existed, joy manifests itself; all beasts rejoice. The children of Sobek, the sons of Neith, the cycle of the gods which dwells in him, are prosperous. No more reservoirs for watering the fields! He makes mankind valiant, enriching some, bestowing his love on others. None commands at the same time as himself. He creates the offerings without the aid of Neith, making mankind for himself with multiform care.

He shines when He issues forth from the darkness, to cause his flocks to prosper. It is his force that gives existence to all things; nothing remains hidden for him. Let men clothe themselves to fill his gardens. He watches over his works, producing the inundation during the night. The associate of Ptah . . . He causes all his servants to exist, all writings and divine words, and that which He needs in the North.

It is with the words that He penetrates into his dwelling; He issues forth at his pleasure through the magic spells. Your unkindness brings destruction to the fish; it is then that prayer is made for the water of the season; Southern Egypt is seen in the same state as the North. Each one is with his instruments of labor. None remains behind his companions. None clothes himself with garments, The children of the noble put aside their ornaments. His night remains silent, but all is changed by the inundation; it is a healing-balm for all mankind.

Establisher of justice! Mankind desires you, supplicating you to answer their prayers; You answer them by the inundation! Men offer the first-fruits of corn; all the gods adore you! The birds descend not on the soil. It is believed that with your hand of gold you make bricks of silver! But we are not nourished on lapis-lazuli; wheat alone gives vigor.

A festal song is raised for you on the harp, with the accompaniment of the hand. Your young men and your children acclaim you and prepare their (long) exercises. You are the august ornament of the earth, letting your bark advance before men, lifting up the heart of women in labor, and loving the multitude of the flocks.

When you shine in the royal city, the rich man is sated with good things, the poor man even disdains the lotus; all that is produced is of the choicest; all the plants exist for your children. If you have refused (to grant) nourishment, the dwelling is silent, devoid of all that is good, the country falls exhausted.

O inundation of the Nile, offerings are made unto you, men are immolated to you, great festivals are instituted for you. Birds are sacrificed to you, gazelles are taken for you in the mountain, pure flames are prepared for you. Sacrifice is mettle to every god as it is made to the Nile. The Nile has made its retreats in Southern Egypt, its name is not known beyond the Tuau. The god manifests not his forms, He baffles all conception.

Men exalt him like the cycle of the gods, they dread him who creates the heat, even him who has made his son the universal master in order to give prosperity to Egypt. Come prosper! Come prosper! O Nile, come prosper! O you who make men to live through his flocks and his flocks through his orchards! Come prosper, come, O Nile, come (and) prosper![3]

Outline

Construct an outline for an essay on the following questions. What was the role of geography in ancient history? What were the main characteristics of Ancient Egypt and Ancient India (Indus River Valley and Vedic Period)?

3 *Hymn to the Nile*, website. Translated by Unknown. Wikisource, https://en.wikisource.org/wiki/Hymn_to_the_Nile. Accessed February 4, 2021.

Lesson 4

The Patriarchs

Vocabulary

Define each term in 5 sentences.

The Bible as a historical document

Abraham

Jacob (Israel)

Quiz

From the Lecture

1. Catholics believe in the inerrancy of the Bible.
   A. True
   B. False

2. What was the result of biblical archeology in the last century?
   A. increased doubt in the existence of the Patriarchs
   B. increased belief in the existence of the Patriarchs
   C. no change in the academic opinion

3. The Dead Sea Scrolls are oldest excerpts of the Bible in existence.
   A. True
   B. False

4. The early Israelites could best be described as:
   A. pastoral.
   B. farmers.
   C. craftsmen.
   D. urbanized.

5. Abraham came originally from what city?
   A. Uruk
   B. Kish
   C. Lagash
   D. Ur

6. What was NOT part of Abraham's convent with God?
   A. circumcision
   B. promise of land
   C. law code
   D. promise of descendants

7. Jacob had twelve children.
   A. True
   B. False

From the Textbook

8. Melchizedek blessed Abraham in the name of:
   A. Jesus.
   B. Elohim.
   C. God Most High.
   D. Yahweh.

9. Who did Isaac visit in Northern Mesopotamia to find a wife?
   A. Laban
   B. Lot
   C. Seth
   D. Jacob

10. Jesus was a descendant of which son of Jacob?
    A. Levi
    B. Joseph
    C. Benjamin
    D. Judah

Writing Assignment

Read the following excerpts from *Genesis*. Write a short 300-word essay answering the following questions. What was the relationship between Abraham and God? How was it different from other religions in Ancient Egypt and Mesopotamia?

Genesis 12:1–7

1 And the Lord said to Abram: Go forth out of thy country, and from thy kindred, and out of thy father's house, and come into the land which I shall show thee. 2 And I will make of thee a great nation,

and I will bless thee, and magnify thy name, and thou shalt be blessed. 3 I will bless them that bless thee, and curse them that curse thee, and IN THEE shall all the kindreds of the earth be blessed. 4 So Abram went out as the Lord had commanded him, and Lot went with him: Abram was seventy-five years old when he went forth from Haran. 5 And he took Sarai his wife, and Lot his brother's son, and all the substance which they had gathered, and the souls which they had gotten in Haran: and they went out to go into the land of Canaan. And when they were come into it. 6 Abram passed through the country unto the place of Shechem, as far as the noble vale: now the Canaanite was at that time in the land. 7 And the Lord appeared to Abram and said to him: To thy seed will I give this land. And he built there an altar to the Lord, who had appeared to him.

Genesis 22:1–19

1 After these things, God tempted Abraham, and said to him: Abraham, Abraham. And he answered: Here I am. 2 He said to him: Take thy only begotten son Isaac, whom thou lovest, and go into the land of vision; and there thou shalt offer him for an holocaust upon one of the mountains which I will show thee. 3 So Abraham rising up in the night, saddled his ass, and took with him two young men, and Isaac his son: and when he had cut wood for the holocaust, he went his way to the place which God had commanded him. 4 And on the third day, lifting up his eyes, he saw the place afar off. 5 And he said to his young men: Stay you here with the ass; I and the boy will go with speed as far as yonder, and after we have worshipped, will return to you. 6 And he took the wood for the holocaust, and laid it upon Isaac his son; and he himself carried in his hands fire and a sword. And as they two went on together. 7 Isaac said to his father: My father. And he answered: What wilt thou, son? Behold, saith he, fire and wood: where is the victim for the holocaust? 8 And Abraham said: God will provide himself a victim for an holocaust, my son. So they went on together. 9 And they came to the place which God had shown him, where he built an altar, and laid the wood in order upon it; and when he had bound Isaac his son, he laid him on the altar upon the pile of wood. 10 And he put forth his hand, and took the sword, to sacrifice his son. 11 And behold, an angel of the Lord from heaven called to him, saying: Abraham, Abraham. And he answered: Here I am. 12 And he said to him: Lay not thy hand upon the boy, neither do thou anything to him: now I know that thou fearest God, and hast not spared thy only begotten son for my sake. 13 Abraham lifted up his eyes, and saw behind his back a ram, amongst the briers, sticking fast by the horns, which he took and offered for a holocaust instead of his son. 14 And he called the name of that place, The Lord seeth. Whereupon, even to this day, it is said: In the mountain the Lord will see. 15 And the angel of the Lord called to Abraham a second time from heaven, saying: 16 By my own self have I sworn, saith the Lord: because thou hast done this thing, and hast not spared thy only begotten son for my sake: 17 I will bless thee, and I will multiply thy seed as the stars of heaven, and as the sand that is by the sea shore; thy seed shall possess the gates of their enemies. 18 And in thy seed shall all the nations of the earth be blessed, because thou hast obeyed my voice. 19 Abraham returned to his young men, and they went to Bersabee together, and he dwelt there.[4]

---

4 *Douay-Rheims Bible,* website. Edited by Richard Challoner. Drbo.org. http://drbo.org/chapter/01012.htm and http://drbo.org/chapter/01022.htm. February 4, 2021.

Outline

Construct an outline for an essay on the following questions. Why can the Bible be used as a historical source? What was the historical significance of Abraham, Isaac, and Jacob (Israel)?

Lesson 5

Moses and the Law

Vocabulary

Define each term in 5 sentences.

The Exodus

Moses

Mosaic Law

Quiz

From the Lecture

1. What foreign group ruled Lower Egypt during the time of Joseph?
    - A. Hittites
    - B. Persian
    - C. Minoans
    - D. Hyksos

2. Amenhotep IV changed his name to:
    - A. Tutankhamun.
    - B. Smenkhkare.
    - C. Akhenaton.
    - D. Meritaten.

3. What thirteenth-century pharaoh was likely in power during the Exodus?
    - A. Seti
    - B. Khufu
    - C. Tutankhamun
    - D. Ramses II

4. What was NOT one of the plagues directed against Egypt?
   A. three days of darkness
   B. blinding sandstorm
   C. boils on men and animals
   D. thunderstorm of hail and fire

5. What did God instruct Moses to build to house the Ark of the Covenant and mark his earthy presence?
   A. an altar
   B. a tent
   C. a temple
   D. a church

6. The Israelites were condemned to wander in the wilderness for forty years because they:
   A. worshiped the gold calf.
   B. complained about the lack of food and water.
   C. did not trust God to deliver to them the Promised Land.
   D. ate the forbidden food.

7. According to Jewish authorities, the Mosaic Law has 473 commandments.
   A. True
   B. False

From the Textbook

8. Which of the following is NOT a city built by the Hebrew slaves?
   A. Thebes
   B. Ramses
   C. Pithom

9. The Israelites took the coast route to the Promised Land to avoid Pharaoh's watch and control.
   A. True
   B. False

10. One piece of evidence that Israelites had not followed the law in the wilderness was:
   A. Joshua had to circumcise the men in his army.
   B. Moses had all the Levites killed.
   C. they lost the Ark of Covenant.
   D. Israelite spies drowned in the Sea of Reeds.

Writing Assignment

Read the following excerpts from *Exodus* and the *Code of Hammurabi*. Write a short 300-word essay answering the following question. What are similarities and differences between the Code of Hammurabi and the Mosaic law?

Code of Hammurabi

When Anu the Sublime, King of the Anunaki, and Bel, the lord of Heaven and earth, who decreed the fate of the land, assigned to Marduk, the over-ruling son of Ea, God of righteousness, dominion over earthly man, and made him great among the Igigi, they called Babylon by his illustrious name, made it great on earth, and founded an everlasting kingdom in it, whose foundations are laid so solidly as those of heaven and earth; then Anu and Bel called by name me, Hammurabi, the exalted prince, who feared God, to bring about the rule of righteousness in the land, to destroy the wicked and the evil-doers; so that the strong should not harm the weak; so that I should rule over the black-headed people like Shamash, and enlighten the land, to further the well-being of mankind. . . .

2. If any one bring an accusation against a man, and the accused go to the river and leap into the river, if he sink in the river his accuser shall take possession of his house. But if the river prove that the accused is not guilty, and he escape unhurt, then he who had brought the accusation shall be put to death, while he who leaped into the river shall take possession of the house that had belonged to his accuser.

3. If any one bring an accusation of any crime before the elders, and does not prove what he has charged, he shall, if it be a capital offense charged, be put to death.

16. If any one receive into his house a runaway male or female slave of the court, or of a freedman, and does not bring it out at the public proclamation of the major domus, the master of the house shall be put to death.

17. If any one find runaway male or female slaves in the open country and bring them to their masters, the master of the slaves shall pay him two shekels of silver.

53. If any one be too lazy to keep his dam in proper condition, and does not so keep it; if then the dam break and all the fields be flooded, then shall he in whose dam the break occurred be sold for money, and the money shall replace the corn which he has caused to be ruined.

157. If any one be guilty of incest with his mother after his father, both shall be burned.

199. If he put out the eye of a man's slave, or break the bone of a man's slave, he shall pay one-half of its value.

200. If a man knock out the teeth of his equal, his teeth shall be knocked out.[5]

Exodus 21:12–20

12 He that strike a man with a will to kill him, shall be put to death. 13 But he that did not lie in wait for him, but God delivered him into his hands: I will appoint thee a place to which he must flee. 14 If a man kill his neighbor on set purpose and by lying in wait for him: thou shalt take him away from my

5 *The Code of Hammurabi*, website. Translated by Leonard William King. Wikisource. https://en.wikisource.org/wiki/Codex_Hammurabi_(King_translation). Accessed February 4, 2021.

altar, that he may die. 15 He that strike his father or mother, shall be put to death.

16 He that shall steal a man, and sell him, being convicted of guilt, shall be put to death. 17 He that curse his father, or mother, shall die the death. 18 If men quarrel, and the one strike his neighbor with a stone or with his fist, and he die not, but keepeth his bed: 19 If he rise again and walk abroad upon his staff, he that struck him shall be quit, yet so that he make restitution for his work, and for his expenses upon the physicians. 20 He that strike his bondman or bondwoman with a rod, and they die under his hands, shall be guilty of the crime.

Exodus 34:11–23

11 Observe all things which this day I command thee: I myself will drive out before thy face the Amorite, and the Canaanite, and the Hethite, and the Pherezite, and the Hevite, and the Jebusite. 12 Beware thou never join in friendship with the inhabitants of that land, which may be thy ruin: 13 But destroy their altars, break their statues, and cut down their groves: 14 Adore not any strange god. The Lord his name is Jealous, he is a jealous God. 15 Make no covenant with the men of those countries lest, when they have committed fornication with their gods, and have adored their idols, some one call thee to eat of the things sacrificed.

16 Neither shalt thou take of their daughters a wife for thy son, lest after they themselves have committed fornication, they make thy sons also to commit fornication with their gods. 17 Thou shalt not make to thyself any molten gods. 18 Thou shalt keep the feast of the unleavened bread. Seven days shalt thou eat unleavened bread, as I commanded thee in the time of the month of the new corn: for in the month of the springtime thou came out from Egypt. 19 All of the male kind, that open the womb, shall be mine. Of all beasts, both of oxen and of sheep, it shall be mine. 20 The firstling of an ass thou shalt redeem with a sheep: but if thou wilt not give a price for it, it shall be slain. The firstborn of thy sons thou shalt redeem: neither shalt thou appear before me empty.

21 Six days shalt thou work, the seventh day thou shalt cease to plough, and to reap. 22 Thou shalt keep the feast of weeks with the first fruits of the corn of thy wheat harvest, and the feast when the time of the year returneth that all things are laid in. 23 Three times in a year all thy males shall appear in the sight of the Almighty Lord the God of Israel.[6]

Outline

Construct an outline for an essay on the following question. What was the role of the exodus and Moses in Ancient Israel?

6 *Douay-Rheims Bible*, website. Edited by Richard Challoner. Drbo.org. http://www.drbo.org/chapter/02021.htm and http://www.drbo.org/chapter/02034.htm. Accessed February 4, 2021.

Lesson 6

The Establishment of a Kingdom and David

Vocabulary

Define each term in 5 sentences.

Joshua

Era of the Judges

David

Quiz

From the Lecture

1. Who was given the military command to conquer the Promised Land?
   A. Joshua
   B. Moses
   C. Aaron
   D. Levi

2. Which of the judges sacrificed his own daughter?
   A. Othniel
   B. Samson
   C. Ehud
   D. Jephthah

3. At the Battle of Aphek, the Philistines captured:
   A. David.
   B. the Gold Throne of Jerusalem.
   C. Samuel.
   D. the Ark of the Covenant.

4. Which one of David's sons revolted and was caught when his head was caught in the branches of a tree?
   A. Absalom
   B. Solomon
   C. Adonijah
   D. Amnon

5. What significant phrase is inscribed on the Dan Tel Stele?
   A. Israel is wasted
   B. House of David
   C. I am that I am
   D. Kingdom of Judah

From the Textbook

6. What Canaanite city attempted to side with Joshua as an ally?
   A. Hazor
   B. Jericho
   C. Makkedah
   D. Gibeon

7. David was from Bethlehem and the tribe of:
   A. Judah.
   B. Benjamin.
   C. Ephraim.
   D. Manasseh.

8. David made Jerusalem his capital after conquering it from the:
   A. Philistines.
   B. Hittites.
   C. Jebusites.
   D. Moabites.

9. Solomon is the son of David and Bathsheba.
   A. True
   B. False

10. What is NOT true about Solomon's temple?
   A. Much of the material and craftsmanship were Phoenician.
   B. It was under construction for seven years.
   C. It replaced a smaller temple built by David.
   D. It housed the Ark of Covenant.

Writing Assignment

Read the following excerpt from 1 Samuel. Write a short 300-word essay answering the following question. What were the dangers of a monarch voiced by Samuel and did any of these warning come to fruition under David and Solomon?

1 Samuel 8:11–22

11 And said: This will be the right of the king, that shall reign over you: He will take your sons, and put them in his chariots, and will make them his horsemen, and his running footmen to run before his chariots, 12 And he will appoint of them to be his tribunes, and centurions, and to plough his fields, and to reap his corn, and to make him arms and chariots. 13 Your daughters also he will take to make him ointments, and to be his cooks, and bakers. 14 And he will take your fields, and your vineyards, and your best oliveyards, and give them to his servants. 15 Moreover he will take the tenth of your corn, and of the revenues of your vineyards, to give his eunuchs and servants.

16 Your servants also and handmaids, and your goodliest young men, and your asses he will take away, and put them to his work. 17 Your flocks also he will tithe, and you shall be his servants. 18 And you shall cry out in that day from the face of the king, whom you have chosen to yourselves. and the Lord will not hear you in that day, because you desired unto yourselves a king. 19 But the people would not hear the voice of Samuel, and they said: Nay: but there shall be a king over us. 20 And we also will be like all nations: and our king shall judge us, and go out before us, and fight our battles for us.

21 And Samuel heard all the words of the people, and rehearsed them in the ears of the Lord. 22 And the Lord said to Samuel: Hearken to their voice, and make them a king. And Samuel said to the men of Israel: Let every man go to his city.[7]

Outline

Construct an outline for an essay on the following question. How did the Israelites conquer the Promised Land and establish a kingdom?

7 *Douay-Rheims Bible,* website. Edited by Richard Challoner. Drbo.org. http://www.drbo.org/chapter/09008.htm. Accessed February 4, 2021.

Lesson 7

STATES IN THE ANCIENT NEAR EAST

Vocabulary

Define each term in 5 sentences.

Hittites

Phoenicians

Assyrians

Quiz

From the Lecture

1. What came after the Bronze Age?
   - A. Copper
   - B. Tin
   - C. Iron
   - D. New Stone

2. Iron is much stronger than bronze.
   - A. True
   - B. False

3. What is NOT an Indo-European language?
   - A. Aramaic
   - B. English
   - C. Sanskrit
   - D. Persian

4. What was one explanation for the military success of the Hittites?
   A. advanced siege weapons
   B. Greek fire
   C. chariots
   D. phalanx system

5. The Phoenicians were known for all the following EXCEPT:
   A. establishing Carthage.
   B. developing an alphabet.
   C. trading purple dye.
   D. defeating the Greeks.

6. Where was the point of origin for the Assyrians?
   A. Northern Mesopotamia
   B. Palestine
   C. Asia Minor
   D. Arabia

7. What was NOT a feature of the Assyrian military conquests?
   A. mass deportations
   B. siege machines
   C. a standing army
   D. the long bow

8. What kingdom did the Assyrian eliminate from history?
   A. Judah
   B. Babylonia
   C. Israel
   D. Egypt

From the Textbook

9. Ashur was the chief god of the Assyrians?
   A. True
   B. False

10. In what battle was Israel allied with Syria and Phoenicia against the Assyrians in 853 BC?
   A. Battle of Damascus
   B. Battle of Qarqar
   C. Battle of Samaria

Writing Assignment

Read the following excerpt from the *Annals of Assure-Nasir-Pal.* Write a short 300-word essay answering the following questions. What was the Assyrian king's view of himself? How did he treat individuals who revolted against him?

Annals of Assure-Nasir-Pal, Column 1

[1.32] I am a King, I am a Lord, I am glorious, I am great, I am mighty, I have arisen, I am Chief, I am a Prince, I am a warrior

[1.33] I am great and I am glorious, Assur-nasir-habal, a mighty King of Assyria, proclaimer of the Moon-god, worshipper of Anu, exalter of Yav, suppliant of the gods

[1.34] am I, servant unyielding, subduing the land of his foeman, a King mighty in battle, destroyer of cities and forests,

[1.35] Chief over opponents, King of the four regions, expeller of his foes, prostrating all his enemies, Prince of a multitude of lands of all Kings

[1.36] Even of all, a Prince subduing those disobedient to him, who is ruling all the multitudes of men. These aspirations to the face of the great gods

[1.37] have gone up; on my destiny steadfastly have they determined; at the wishes of my heart and the uplifting of my hand, Istar, exalted Lady,

[1.38] hath favored me in my intentions, and to the conduct of (my) battles and warfare hath applied her heart. In those days I Assur-nasir-pal, glorious Prince, worshipper of the great gods. . . .

[1.79] . . . To Suri which is in Bit-Halupe I drew near;

[1.80] the fear of the approach of Assur my Lord overwhelmed them; the great men and the multitudes of the city, for the saving of their lives, coming up after me,

[1.81] submitted to my yoke; some slain, some living, some tongue-less I made: Ahiyababa son of Lamamana

[1.82] whom from Bit-Adini they had fetched, I captured; in the valor of my heart and the steadfastness of my soldiers I besieged the city; the soldiers, rebels all,

[1.83] were taken prisoners; the nobles to the principal palace of his land I caused to send; his silver, his gold, his treasure, his riches, copper

[1.84] (?)tin, *kams, tabhani, hariati* of copper, choice copper in abundance, alabaster and ironstone of large size

[1.85] the treasures of his harem, his daughters and the wives of the rebels with their treasures, and the gods with their treasures,

[1.86] precious stones of the land of . . . , his swift chariot, his horses, the harness, his chariot-yoke, trappings for horses, coverings for men,

[1.87] vestments of wool, vestments of linen, handsome altars of cedar, handsome . . . , bowls of cedar-wood

[1.88] beautiful black coverings, beautiful purple coverings, carpets, his oxen, his sheep, his abundant spoil, which like the stars of heaven could not be reckoned,

[1.89] I carried off; Aziel as my lieutenant over them I placed; a trophy along the length of the great gate I erected: the rebellious nobles

[1.90] who had revolted against me and whose skins I had stripped off, I made into a trophy: some in the middle of the pile I left to decay; some on the top

[1.91] of the pile on stakes I impaled; some by the side of the pile I placed in order on stakes; many within view of my land

[1.92] I flayed; their skins on the walls I arranged; of the officers of the King's officer, rebels, the limbs I cut off;

[1.93] I brought Ahiyababa to Nineveh; I flayed, him and fastened his skin to the wall; laws and edicts

[1.94] over Lakie I established. While I was staying in Suri the tribute of the Princes of Lakie throughout the whole of them,

[1.95] silver, gold, tin, copper, *kam* of copper, oxen, sheep, vestments of wool and linen, as tribute

[1.96] and gift, I defined and imposed upon them. In those days, the tribute of Khayani of the city of Hindanai, silver,

[1.97] gold, tin, copper, amu-stone, alabaster blocks, beautiful black (and) lustrous coverings I received as tribute from him. In those days an enlarged image

[1.98] of my Royalty I made; edicts and decrees upon it I wrote; in the midst of his palace I put it up; of stone my tablets I made;

[1.99] the decrees of my throne upon it I wrote; in the great gate I fixed them, in the date of this year which takes its name from me, in honor of Assur my Lord and Ninip who uplifts my feet.[8]

Outline

Construct an outline for an essay on the following question: How did the Hittites, Phoenicians, and Assyrians expand, and what were some characteristics of their states?

8 *Annals of Assure-Nasir-Pal,* website. Translated by Rev. J. M. Rodwell, M.A. Marquette University. http://mcadams.posc.mu.edu/txt/ah/Assyria/Inscra02.html. (Accessed 2/16/2021).

Lesson 8

A Divided Kingdom

Vocabulary

Define each term in 5 sentences.

Kingdom of Israel

Kingdom of Judah

Prophets (Isaiah and Jeremiah)

Quiz

From the Lecture

1. The Kingdom of Israel was ruled by descendants of King David.
    - A. True
    - B. False

2. The Kingdom of Judah contained the tribes of Judah and Manasseh.
    - A. True
    - B. False

3. What was NOT one of the reasons Elijah confronted Ahab?
    - A. killing the priests of the temple
    - B. worshipping Baal
    - C. killing Naboth for his vineyard

4. Jonah was sent by God to what city?
    - A. Thebes
    - B. Ashur
    - C. Nineveh
    - D. Samaria

5. In the book of Hosea, the relationship between God and Israel is likened to a:
    A. father and son.
    B. master and servant.
    C. two individuals in love with each other.
    D. husband and adulterous wife.

From the Textbook

6. Jeroboam created shrines to rival Jerusalem at Dan and:
    A. Bethel.
    B. Samaria.
    C. Carmel.
    D. Shechem.

7. Jezebel's father was the king of what Phoenician city?
    A. Sidon
    B. Carthage
    C. Minoa
    D. Tyre

8. How did Queen Athaliah attempt to place herself on the throne of David?
    A. marry the high priest
    B. kill all her sons and grandsons
    C. conspire with Assyrian forces
    D. led the army to victory over the kings of Damascus

9. How many inhabitants of Samaria were deported by Sargon II?
    A. 12,450
    B. 16,700
    C. 21,050
    D. 27,290

10. Where did Isaiah predict that a child would appear named "Wonderful Counselor, Mighty God, Everlasting Father, Prince of Peace"?
    A. Bethlehem
    B. Nazareth
    C. Jerusalem
    D. Galilee

Writing Assignment

Read the following excerpt from *Isaiah*. Write a short 300-word essay answering the following question. How was monotheism described by Isaiah?

Isaiah 44:6–25

6 Thus saith the Lord the king of Israel, and his redeemer the Lord of hosts: I am the first, and I am the last, and besides me there is no God. 7 Who is like to me? let him call and declare: and let him set before me the order, since I appointed the ancient people: and the things to come, and that shall be hereafter, let them shew unto them. 8 Fear ye not, neither be ye troubled, from that time I have made thee to hear, and have declared: you are my witnesses. Is there a God besides me, a maker, whom I have not known? 9 The makers of idols are all of them nothing, and their best beloved things shall not profit them. They are their witnesses, that they do not see, nor understand, that they may be ashamed. 10 Who hath formed a god, and made a graven thing that is profitable for nothing?

11 Behold, all the partakers thereof shall be confounded: for the makers are men: they shall all assemble together, they shall stand and fear, and shall be confounded together. 12 The smith hath wrought with his file, with coals, and with hammers he hath formed it, and hath wrought with the strength of his arm: he shall hunger and faint, he shall drink no water, and shall be weary. 13 The carpenter hath stretched out his rule, he hath formed it with a plane: he hath made it with corners, and hath fashioned it round with the compass: and he hath made the image of a man as it were a beautiful man dwelling in a house. 14 He hath cut down cedars, taken the holm, and the oak that stood among the trees of the forest: he hath planted the pine tree, which the rain hath nourished. 15 And it hath served men for fuel: he took thereof, and warmed himself: and he kindled it, and baked bread: but of the rest he made a god, and adored it: he made a graven thing, and bowed down before it.

16 Part of it he burnt with fire, and with part of it he dressed his meat: he boiled pottage, and was filled, and was warmed, and said: Aha, I am warm, I have seen the fire. 17 But the residue thereof he made a god, and a graven thing for himself: he boweth down before it, and adoreth it, and prayeth unto it, saying: Deliver me, for thou art my God. 18 They have not known, nor understood: for their eyes are covered that they may not see, and that they may not understand with their heart. 19 They do not consider in their mind, nor know, nor have the thought to say: I have burnt part of it in the fire, and I have baked bread upon the coals thereof: I have broiled flesh and have eaten, and of the residue thereof shall I make an idol? shall I fall down before the stock of a tree? 20 Part thereof is ashes: his foolish heart adoreth it, and he will not save his soul, nor say: Perhaps there is a lie in my right hand.

21 Remember these things, O Jacob, and Israel, for thou art my servant. I have formed thee, thou art my servant, O Israel, forget me not. 22 I have blotted out thy iniquities as a cloud, and thy sins as a mist: return to me, for I have redeemed thee. 23 Give praise, O ye heavens, for the Lord hath shewn mercy: shout with joy, ye ends of the earth: ye mountains, resound with praise, thou, O forest, and every tree therein: for the Lord hath redeemed Jacob, and Israel shall be glorified. 24 Thus saith the Lord thy redeemer, and thy maker, from the womb: I am the Lord, that make all things, that alone stretch out the heavens, that establish the earth, and there is none with me. 25 That make void the tokens of diviners, and make the soothsayers mad. That turn the wise backward, and that, make their knowledge foolish.[9]

---

9 *Douay-Rheims Bible,* website. Edited by Richard Challoner. Drbo.org. http://drbo.org/chapter/27044.htm. Accessed February 23, 2021.

Outline

Construct an outline for an essay on the following questions. What were the events that led to the division of the kingdom? What were the main characteristics of the Kingdom of Israel and the Kingdom of Judah?

Lesson 9

Neo-Babylonians and the Persians

Vocabulary

Define each term in 5 sentences.

Nebuchadnezzar II

Cyrus the Great

Persian Empire

Quiz

From the Lecture

1. King Hezekiah was faithful to Yahweh and purged foreign gods from the temple.
    A. True
    B. False

2. What was the purpose of the Siloam tunnel?
    A. to escape the city during a fire
    B. to irrigate fields with fresh water
    C. to mine under the walls of Jerusalem causing them to collapse
    D. to bring in fresh water during a siege

3. The city of Jerusalem and temple were destroyed after the first Neo-Babylonian siege in 598/7.
    A. True
    B. False

4. The Persians were related to what other ancient nation?
    A. Assyrians
    B. Medes
    C. Babylonians
    D. Greeks

5. Who was the son of Cyrus the Great who conquered Egypt?
   A. Darius I
   B. Darius II
   C. Cambyses II
   D. Xerxes

From the Textbook

6. According to St. Jerome and modern scholars, what "book of laws" was rediscovered in the temple during the reign of King Josiah?
   A. Exodus
   B. Leviticus
   C. Numbers
   D. Deuteronomy

7. What group was NOT part of the coalition that finally defeated the Assyrians at Nineveh?
   A. Egyptians
   B. Medes
   C. Babylonians
   D. Umman-manda

8. Who was the most influential individual in the religion of the Persians?
   A. Daniel
   B. Zoroaster
   C. Buddha
   D. Plato

9. What did the Jews do after returning to the Promised Land from Babylon?
   A. rebuild the temple
   B. massacre the Samaritans
   C. establish an independent kingdom
   D. flee to Egypt looking for grain

10. What story did Darius construct to come to power?
    A. He was a lost son of Cyrus.
    B. The king was really an imposter.
    C. Zoroaster anointed him king.
    D. He inherited the seal of the king.

Writing Assignment

Read the following excerpt from Xenophon's *The Education of Cyrus*. Write a short 300-word essay answering the following questions. How did King Cyrus treat his subject? What impact did his treatment have on their loyalty and respect for him?

The Education of Cyrus Book 5, Chapter 3

(46) So the officers went to their quarters, and as they went they talked of Cyrus, and what a marvelous memory he had, always naming each officer as he assigned him his post. (47) The fact was Cyrus took special pains over this: it struck him as odd that a mere mechanic could know the names of all his tools, and a physician the names of all his instruments, but a general be such a simpleton that he could not name his own officers, the very tools he had to depend on each time he wanted to seize a point or fortify a post or infuse courage or inspire terror. Moreover it seemed to him only courteous to address a man by name when he wished to honor him. (48) And he was sure that the man who feels he is personally known to his commander is more eager to be seen performing some noble feat of arms, and more careful to refrain from all that is unseemly and base. (49) Cyrus thought it would be quite foolish for him to give his orders in the style of certain householders: "Somebody fetch the water, some one split the wood." (50) After a command of that kind, every one looks at every one else, and no one carries it out, every one is to blame, and no one is ashamed or afraid, because there are so many beside himself. Therefore Cyrus always named the officers whenever he gave an order.

The Education of Cyrus Book 8, Chapter 2

(C.2) In the first place he never lost an opportunity of showing kindliness wherever he could, convinced that just as it is not easy to love those who hate us, so it is scarcely possible to feel enmity for those who love us and wish us well. (2) So long as he had lacked the power to confer benefits by wealth, all he could do then was to show his personal care for his comrades and his soldiers, to labor in their behalf, manifest his joy in their good fortune and his sympathy in their sorrows, and try to win them in that way. But when the time came for the gifts of wealth, he realized that of all the kindnesses between man and man none come with a more natural grace than the gifts of meat and drink. (3) Accordingly he arranged that his table should be spread every day for many guests in exactly the same way as for himself; and all that was set before him, after he and his guests had dined, he would send out to his absent friends, in token of affection and remembrance. He would include those who had won his approval by their work on guard, or in attendance on himself, or in any other service, letting them see that no desire to please him could ever escape his eyes. (4) He would show the same honor to any servant he wished to praise; and he had all the food for them placed at his own board, believing this would win their fidelity, as it would a dog's. Or, if he wished some friend of his to be courted by the people, he would single him out for such gifts; even to this day the world will pay court to those who have dishes sent them from the Great King's table, thinking they must be in high favor at the palace and can get things done for others. But no doubt there was another reason for the pleasure in such gifts, and that was the sheer delicious taste of the royal meats. the bread, and not all of it either, for the loaves must be of different kinds, and it will be quite enough if the baker can serve up one kind to perfection—it is obvious, I think, that in this way a far higher standard of excellence will be attained in every branch of the work.[10]

---

10 Xenophon. *Cyropaedia (The Education of Cyrus), ebook.* Translated by Henry Graham Dakyns. Edited by F. M. Stawell. Project Gutenberg. https://www.gutenberg.org/files/2085/2085-h/2085-h.htm. (Accessed February 23, 2021)

Outline

Construct an outline for an essay on the following question. What were the difference and similarities between the Neo-Babylonians and Persians with particular attention given to the monarchs and treatment of the Jews?

Lesson 10

The Rise of the Greeks

Vocabulary

Define each term in 5 sentences.

Minoans

Mycenaeans

Homer

Quiz

From the Lecture

1. Classical antiquity is centered on what two civilizations?
    - A. Egypt and Mesopotamia
    - B. Egypt and Persia
    - C. Egypt and Israel
    - D. Greece and Rome

2. Where did advanced civilization first appear in the Greek world?
    - A. Crete
    - B. Sparta
    - C. Athens
    - D. Ionia

3. The name Minoan is derived from the name of:
    - A. their language.
    - A. a legendary king.
    - A. their largest palace.
    - A. their chief god.

4. Which of the following is NOT true about the Mycenaean writing script.
    A. It is Greek.
    B. It is called Linear B.
    C. It was used by Aristotle and Plato.
    D. It has been deciphered by modern scholars.

5. Where does the revival of Greek writing represented by Homer take place?
    A. Athens
    B. Sparta
    C. Crete
    D. Ionian Coast

6. One of the central themes of the Iliad is the feud between Achilles and Agamemnon.
    A. True
    B. False

7. The Odyssey is the story of the Mycenean Greek states and their war against Troy.
    A. True
    B. False

8. Who was the wife of Zeus and queen of the Olympian gods?
    A. Hera
    B. Athena
    C. Demeter
    D. Aphrodite

From the Textbook

9. Who formulated the main ideas of the Jain religion?
    A. Buddha
    B. Mahavira
    C. Zoroaster
    D. Huangdi

10. What best describes the followers of the Way of Lao Tzu?
    A. inhuman treatment of others
    B. public service out of duty
    C. withdrawn from public life
    D. life of hedonism

Writing Assignment

Read the following excerpt from Homer's *Iliad*. Write a short 300-word essay answering the following questions. What changed Achilles's mind about joining the war against Troy? What does this reveal about the warrior culture of the period?

Book 18

As he was thus pondering, the son of Nestor came up to him and told his sad tale, weeping bitterly the while. "Alas," he cried, "son of noble Peleus, I bring you bad tidings, would indeed that they were untrue. Patroclus has fallen, and a fight is raging about his naked body—for Hector holds his armour."

A dark cloud of grief fell upon Achilles as he listened. He filled both hands with dust from off the ground, and poured it over his head, disfiguring his comely face, and letting the refuse settle over his shirt so fair and new. He flung himself down all huge and hugely at full length, and tore his hair with his hands. The bondswomen whom Achilles and Patroclus had taken captive screamed aloud for grief, beating their breasts, and with their limbs failing them for sorrow. Antilochus bent over him the while, weeping and holding both his hands as he lay groaning for he feared that he might plunge a knife into his own throat. Then Achilles gave a loud cry and his mother heard him as she was sitting in the depths of the sea by the old man her father, whereon she screamed, and all the goddesses daughters of Nereus that dwelt at the bottom of the sea, came gathering round her. . . .

Achilles groaned and answered, "Mother, Olympian Jove has indeed vouchsafed me the fulfilment of my prayer, but what boots it to me, seeing that my dear comrade Patroclus has fallen—he whom I valued more than all others, and loved as dearly as my own life? I have lost him; aye, and Hector when he had killed him stripped the wondrous armour, so glorious to behold, which the gods gave to Peleus when they laid you in the couch of a mortal man. Would that you were still dwelling among the immortal sea-nymphs, and that Peleus had taken to himself some mortal bride. For now you shall have grief infinite by reason of the death of that son whom you can never welcome home—nay, I will not live nor go about among mankind unless Hector fall by my spear, and thus pay me for having slain Patroclus son of Menoetius."

Thetis wept and answered, "Then, my son, is your end near at hand—for your own death awaits you full soon after that of Hector."

Then said Achilles in his great grief, "I would die here and now, in that I could not save my comrade. He has fallen far from home, and in his hour of need my hand was not there to help him. What is there for me? Return to my own land I shall not, and I have brought no saving neither to Patroclus nor to my other comrades of whom so many have been slain by mighty Hector; I stay here by my ships a bootless burden upon the earth, I, who in fight have no peer among the Achaeans, though in council there are better than I. Therefore, perish strife both from among gods and men, and anger, wherein even a righteous man will harden his heart—which rises up in the soul of a man like smoke, and the taste thereof is sweeter than drops of honey. Even so has Agamemnon angered me. And yet—so be it, for it is over; I will force my soul into subjection as I needs must; I will go; I will pursue Hector who has slain him whom I loved so dearly, and will then abide my doom when it may please Jove and the other gods to send it. Even Hercules, the best beloved of Jove—even he could not escape the hand of death, but fate and Juno's fierce anger laid him low, as I too shall lie when I am dead if a like doom awaits me. Till then I will win fame, and will bid Trojan and Dardanian women wring tears from their tender cheeks with both their hands in the grievousness of their great sorrow; thus shall they know that he who has held aloof so long will hold aloof no longer. Hold me not back, therefore, in the love you bear me, for you shall not move me."[11]

---

11 Homer. *Iliad, ebook*. Translated by Samuel Butler. Project Gutenberg. http://www.gutenberg.org/files/2199/2199-h/2199-h.htm. (Accessed February 26, 2021).

Outline

Construct an outline for an essay on the following question. What were the Minoan, Mycenaean, and literary roots (Homer) of Greek Civilization?

Lesson 11

Greeks and War

Vocabulary

Define each term in 5 sentences.

Sparta

Athens

Persian Wars

Quiz

From the Lecture

1. The heavily armed foot soldiers of Ancient Greece were known as:
    - A. legionaries.
    - B. phalanx.
    - C. immortals.
    - D. hoplites.

2. In Sparta, what the role of the helots?
    - A. free merchants
    - B. warriors
    - C. enslaved farmers
    - D. priests

3. How many kings ruled in Sparta?
    - A. none
    - B. one
    - C. two
    - D. three

4. Who reformed the constitution of Athens to have ten tribes?
    A. Cleisthenes
    B. Peisistratos
    C. Solon
    D. Draco

5. What was the decisive naval battle against the forces of Xerxes?
    A. Thermopylae
    B. Salamis
    C. Plataea
    D. Marathon

6. What best describes Athens's treatment of its allies after the defeat Persia?
    A. Athens provided generous rewards.
    B. Athens shared the victory and glory.
    C. Athens controlled them and required tribute.
    D. Athens ignored them.

From the Textbook

7. Where did Greeks revolt that triggered multiple wars with Persia?
    A. Sicily
    B. Ionia
    C. Athens
    D. Macedon

8. What battle thwarted the first Persian invasion under Darius?
    A. Thermopylae
    B. Salamis
    C. Plataea
    D. Marathon

9. What financed the expansion of the Athenian fleet after the first Persian invasion?
    A. silver mine
    B. new taxes
    C. tribute from the Delian League
    D. peace settlement from Sparta

10. Nehemiah was responsible for what improvement to Jerusalem?
    A. retaking it from the Greeks
    B. rebuilding the walls
    C. rebuilding the temple
    D. building a palace

Writing Assignment

Read the following excerpt from Pericles's *Funeral Oration*. Write a short 300-word essay answering the following question. What made Athens unique according to Pericles?

Funeral Oration

For we enjoy a form of government which does not copy the laws of our neighbors; but we are ourselves rather a pattern to others than imitators of them. In name, from its not being administered for the benefit of the few, but of the many, it is called a democracy; but with regard to its laws, all enjoy equality, as concerns their private differences; while with regard to public rank, according as each man has reputation for anything, he is preferred for public honors, not so much from consideration of party, as of merit; nor, again, on the ground of poverty, while he is able to do the state any good service, is he prevented by the obscurity of his position. We are liberal then in our public administration; and with regard to mutual jealousy of our daily pursuits, we are not angry with our neighbor, if he does anything to please himself; nor wear on our countenance offensive looks, which tho harmless, are yet unpleasant. While, however, in private matters we live together agreeably, in public matters, under the influence of fear, we most carefully abstain from transgression, through our obedience to those who are from time to time in office, and to the laws; especially such of them as are enacted for the benefit of the injured, and such as, tho unwritten, bring acknowledged disgrace [on those who break them]. . . .

In the studies of war also we differ from our enemies in the following respects: We throw our city open to all, and never, by the expulsion of strangers, exclude anyone from either learning or observing things, by seeing which unconcealed any of our enemies might gain an advantage; for we trust not so much to preparations and stratagems, as to our own valor for daring deeds. Again, as to our modes of education, *they* aim at the acquisition of a manly character, by laborious training from their very youth; while *we*, tho living at our ease, no less boldly advance to meet equal dangers. As a proof of this, the Lacedæmonians never march against our country singly, but with all [their confederates] together: while we, generally speaking, have no difficulty in conquering in battle upon hostile ground those who are standing up in defense of their own. And no enemy ever yet encountered our whole united force, through our attending at the same time to our navy, and sending our troops by land on so many different services: but wherever they have engaged with any part of it. if they conquer only some of us, they boast that we were all routed by them; and if they are conquered, they say it was by all that they were beaten. And yet if with careless ease rather than with laborious practice, and with a courage which is the result not so much of laws as of natural disposition, we are willing to face danger, we have the advantage of not suffering beforehand from coming troubles, and of proving ourselves, when we are involved in them, no less bold than those who are always toiling; so that our country is worthy of admiration in these respects, and in others besides. . . .

In short, I say that both the whole city is a school for Greece, and that, in my opinion, the same individual would among us provide himself qualified for the most varied kinds of action, and with the most graceful versatility. And that this is not mere vaunting language for the occasion, so much as actual truth, the very power of the state, which we have won by such habits, affords a proof. For it is the only country at the present time that, when brought to the test, proves superior to its fame; and the only one that neither gives to the enemy who has attacked us any cause for indignation at being worsted by such opponents, nor to him who is subject to us room for finding fault, as not being ruled by men who are worthy of empire. But we shall be admired both by present and future generations as having exhibited our power with great proofs, and by no means without evidence; and as having no further need, either of Homer to praise us or anyone else who might charm for the moment by his verses, while the truth of the facts would mar the idea formed of them; but as having compelled every sea and land to become accessible to our daring, and everywhere established everlasting records, whether of evil or of good. It was for such a country then that these men, nobly resolving not to have it taken from them, fell fighting; and every one of their survivors may well be willing to suffer in its behalf.[12]

Outline

Construct an outline for an essay on the following questions. What were the political systems of Athens and Sparta? What were the main characteristics of the Greco-Persian Wars and the Peloponnesian War?

---

12 Pericles. *Funeral Oration, website.* Translated by Henry Dale. Wikisource. https://en.wikisource.org/wiki/The_World%27s_Famous_Orations/Volume_1/On_Those_Who_Died_in_the_War. (Accessed 3/4/2021).

Lesson 12

Greek Culture

Vocabulary

Define each term in 5 sentences.

Greek Philosophers

Greek Historians

Greek Tragedies

Quiz

From the Lecture

1. Thales claimed that fire was the primal substance.
   - A. True
   - B. False

2. Democritus argued that everything was composed of atoms.
   - A. True
   - B. False

3. Who was sentenced to death in Athens in 399 BC?
   - A. Plato
   - B. Aristotle
   - C. Socrates
   - D. Pythagoras

4. Aristotle did NOT compose any work in what field?
   - A. Political Science
   - B. Physics
   - C. Sculpture
   - D. Logic

5. Who is considered the father of history?
    A. Aristotle
    B. Plato
    C. Thucydides
    D. Herodotus

6. Thucydides fought in the Peloponnesian War.
    A. True
    B. False

7. What is the Greek meaning of the word "tragedy"?
    A. old theater
    B. cult dance
    C. goat song
    D. dance of the gods

8. Which one of the following is not a Greek tragedian?
    A. Phidias
    B. Sophocles
    C. Euripides
    D. Aeschylus

9. The Parthenon is dedicated to what Greek deity?
    A. Zeus
    B. Athena
    C. Hermes
    D. Aphrodite

10. What best describes the Greek agora?
    A. a colonnaded walkway for shops
    B. a meeting space carved into a hillside
    C. an open space used for public gatherings
    D. a building used to worship the gods

Writing Assignment

Read the following excerpt from Plato's *The Republic.* Write a short 300-word essay answering the following question. What is the meaning of the allegory of the cave?

The Republic, Book VII

Behold! Human beings living in an underground den, which has a mouth open towards the light and reaching all along the den; here they have been from their childhood, and have their legs and necks chained so that they cannot move, and can only see before them, being prevented by the chains from turning round their heads. Above and behind them a fire is blazing at a distance, and between the fire and the prisoners there is a raised way; and you will see, if you look, a low wall built along the way, like the screen which marionette players have in front of them, over which they show the puppets.

I see.

And do you see, I said, men passing along the wall carrying all sorts of vessels, and statues and figures of animals made of wood and stone and various materials, which appear over the wall? Some of them are talking, others silent.

You have shown me a strange image, and they are strange prisoners.

Like ourselves, I replied; and they see only their own shadows, or the shadows of one another, which the fire throws on the opposite wall of the cave?

True, he said; how could they see anything but the shadows if they were never allowed to move their heads?

And of the objects which are being carried in like manner they would only see the shadows?

Yes, he said.

And if they were able to converse with one another, would they not suppose that they were naming what was actually before them?

Very true.

And suppose further that the prison had an echo which came from the other side, would they not be sure to fancy when one of the passers-by spoke that the voice which they heard came from the passing shadow?

No question, he replied.

To them, I said, the truth would be literally nothing but the shadows of the images.

That is certain.

And now look again and see what will naturally follow if the prisoners are released and disabused of their error. At first, when any of them is liberated and compelled suddenly to stand up and turn his neck round and walk and look towards the light, he will suffer sharp pains; the glare will distress him, and he will be unable to see the realities of which in his former state he had seen the shadows; and then conceive some one saying to him, that what he saw before was an illusion, but that now, when he is approaching nearer to being and his eye is turned towards more real existence, he has a clearer vision,—what will be his reply? And you may further imagine that his instructor is pointing to the objects as they pass and requiring him to name them,—will he not be perplexed? Will he not fancy that the shadows which he formerly saw are truer than the objects which are now shown to him?

Far truer.

And if he is compelled to look straight at the light, will he not have a pain in his eyes which will make him turn away to take and take in the objects of vision which he can see, and which he will conceive to be in reality clearer than the things which are now being shown to him?

True, he said.

And suppose once more, that he is reluctantly dragged up a steep and rugged ascent, and held fast until he's forced into the presence of the sun himself, is he not likely to be pained and irritated? When he approaches the light his eyes will be dazzled, and he will not be able to see anything at all of what are now called realities.

Not all in a moment, he said.

He will require to grow accustomed to the sight of the upper world. And first he will see the shadows best, next the reflections of men and other objects in the water, and then the objects themselves; then he will gaze upon the light of the moon and the stars and the spangled heaven; and he will see the sky and the stars by night better than the sun or the light of the sun by day?

Certainly.

Last of he will be able to see the sun, and not mere reflections of him in the water, but he will see him in his own proper place, and not in another; and he will contemplate him as he is.

Certainly.

He will then proceed to argue that this is he who gives the season and the years, and is the guardian of all that is in the visible world, and in a certain way the cause of all things which he and his fellows have been accustomed to behold?

Clearly, he said, he would first see the sun and then reason about him.

And when he remembered his old habitation, and the wisdom of the den and his fellow-prisoners, do you not suppose that he would felicitate himself on the change, and pity them?

Certainly, he would.

And if they were in the habit of conferring honours among themselves on those who were quickest to observe the passing shadows and to remark which of them went before, and which followed after, and which were together; and who were therefore best able to draw conclusions as to the future, do you think that he would care for such honours and glories, or envy the possessors of them? Would he not say with Homer, Better to be the poor servant of a poor master, and to endure anything, rather than think as they do and live after their manner?

Yes, he said, I think that he would rather suffer anything than entertain these false notions and live in this miserable manner.[13]

Outline

Construct an outline for an essay on the following question. What are the contributions of Ancient Greece in philosophy, history, and the arts?

13 Plato. *The Republic. Gutenberg Edition.* Translated by Benjamin Jowett. Wikisource. https://en.wikisource.org/wiki/The_Republic_(Gutenberg_edition)/Book_VII. (Accessed on March 18, 2021).

Lesson 13

Alexander the Great

Vocabulary

Define each term in 5 sentences.

Philip II of Macedon

Alexander the Great

Alexander the Great's Conquest of Persia

Quiz

From the Lecture

1. Where did Philip II of Macedon spend some of his childhood as a hostage?
   A. Thebes
   B. Athens
   C. Persia
   D. Sparta

2. Philip was assassinated by:
   A. Alexander.
   B. his wife, Olympias.
   C. his bodyguard.
   D. a Spartan nationalist.

3. Who served as the tutor of Alexander?
   A. Socrates
   B. Aristotle
   C. Plato
   D. Euripides

4. Alexander failed to conquer India because:
    A. war elephants.
    B. he had to put down a rebellion in Persia.
    C. he was defeated by Magda.
    D. his troops wanted to return home.

5. Alexander did all the following EXCEPT:
    A. found new Hellenistic cities.
    B. take Asian wives.
    C. conquer Arabia.
    D. become venerated as a god in Egypt.

From the Textbook

6. What happened to Xenophon's Greek army in the Persian Empire?
    A. They were captured.
    B. They were killed.
    C. They established a colony.
    D. They escaped.

7. What was NOT a military advancement initiated by Philip?
    A. phalanx using the sarissa
    B. companion cavalry
    C. the Immortals
    D. royal shield-bearers

8. How did Alexander neutralize the naval threat of the Persians?
    A. He captured all the port cities.
    B. He bribed the admirals.
    C. He built a navy.
    D. He allied with Carthage.

9. What new military challenge did Alexander defeat in India?
    A. Scythian chariots
    B. war elephants
    C. Hun calvary
    D. Chinese guns

10. Who controlled Alexander's empire after his death?
    A. his brother
    B. his son
    C. his generals
    D. his mother

Writing Assignment

Read the following excerpt from Arrian of Nicomedia's *The Anabasis of Alexander.* Write a short 300-word essay answering the following questions. Why and how did Alexander capture Tyre? What does this story demonstrate about the military mind of Alexander?

Chapter XVII. Speech of Alexander to His Officers.

"Friends and allies, I see that an expedition to Egypt will not be safe for us, so long as the Persians retain the sovereignty of the sea; nor is it a safe course, both for other reasons, and especially looking at the state of matters in Greece, for us to pursue Darius, leaving in our rear the city of Tyre itself in doubtful allegiance, and Egypt and Cyprus in the occupation of the Persians. I am apprehensive lest while we advance with our forces towards Babylon and in pursuit of Darius, the Persians should again forsooth conquer the maritime districts, and transfer the war into Greece with a larger army, considering that the Lacedaemonians are now waging war against us without disguise, and the city of Athens is restrained for the present rather by fear than by any good-will towards us. But if Tyre were captured, the whole of Phoenicia would be in our possession, and the fleet of the Phoenicians, which is the most numerous and the best in the Persian navy, would in all probability come over to us. For the Phoenician sailors and marines will not put to sea in order to incur danger on behalf of others, when their own cities are occupied by us. After this, Cyprus will either yield to us without delay, or will be captured with ease at the mere arrival of a naval force; and then navigating the sea with the ships from Macedonia in conjunction with those of the Phoenicians, Cyprus at the same time coming over to us, we shall acquire the absolute sovereignty of the sea, and at the same time an expedition into Egypt will become an easy matter for us. After we have brought Egypt into subjection, no anxiety about Greece and our own land will any longer remain, and we shall be able to undertake the expedition to Babylon with safety in regard to affairs at home, and at the same time with greater reputation, in consequence of having cut off from the Persian empire all the maritime provinces and all the land this side of the Euphrates."

Chapter XVIII. Siege of Tyre.—Construction of a Mole From the Mainland to the Island.

Certainly, the siege of Tyre appeared to be a great enterprise; for the city was an island and fortified all round with lofty walls. Moreover naval operations seemed at that time more favourable to the Tyrians, both because the Persians still possessed the sovereignty of the sea and many ships were still remaining with the citizens themselves. However, as these arguments of his had prevailed, he resolved to construct a mole from the mainland to the city. The place is a narrow strait full of pools; and the part of it near the mainland is shallow water and muddy, but the part near the city itself, where was the deepest part of the channel, was the depth of about three fathoms. But there was an abundant supply of stones and wood, which they put on the top of the stones. Stakes were easily fixed down firmly in the mud, which itself served as a cement to the stones to hold them firm. The zeal of the Macedonians in the work was great, and it was increased by the presence of Alexander himself, who took the lead in everything, now rousing the men to exertion by speech, and now by presents of money, lightening the labour of those who were toiling more than their fellows from the desire of gaining praise for their exertions. As long as the mole was being constructed near the mainland, the work made easy and rapid progress, as the material was poured into a small depth of water, and there was no one to hinder them; but when they began to approach the deeper water, and at the same time came near the city itself, they suffered severely, being assailed with missiles from the walls, which were lofty, inasmuch as they had been expressly equipped for work rather than for fighting. Moreover, as the Tyrians still retained command of the sea, they kept on sailing with their triremes to various parts of the mole, and made it impossible in many places for the Macedonians to pour in the material. But the latter erected two towers upon the mole, which they had now projected over a long stretch of sea, and upon these towers they placed engines of war. Skins and prepared hides served as coverings in front of them, to prevent them being struck by fire-bearing missiles from the wall, and at the same time to be a screen against arrows to those who were working. It was likewise intended that the Tyrians who might sail near to injure the men engaged in the construction of the mole should not retire easily, being assailed by missiles from the towers.

Chapter XXIV. Capture of Tyre.

The main body of the Tyrians deserted the wall when they saw it in the enemy's possession; and rallying opposite what was called the chapel of Agenor, they there turned round to resist the Macedonians. Against these Alexander advanced with his shield-bearing guards, destroyed the men who fought there, and pursued those who fled. Great was the slaughter also made both by those who were now occupying the city from the harbour and by the regiment of Coenus, which had also entered it. For the Macedonians were now for the most part advancing full of rage, being angry both at the length of the siege and also because the Tyrians, having captured some of their men sailing from Sidon, had conveyed them to the top of their wall, so that the deed might be visible from the camp, and after slaughtering them, had cast their bodies into the sea. About 8,000 of the Tyrians were killed; and of the Macedonians, besides Admetus, who had proved himself a valiant man, being the first to scale the wall, twenty of the shield-bearing guards were killed in the assault on that occasion. In the whole siege about 400 Macedonians were slain. Alexander gave an amnesty to all those who fled for refuge into the temple of Heracles; among them being most of the Tyrian magistrates, including the king Azemilcus, as well as certain envoys from the Carthaginians, who had come to their mother-city to attend the sacrifice in honour of Heracles, according to an ancient custom. The rest of the prisoners were reduced to slavery; all the Tyrians and mercenary troops, to the number of about 30,000, who had been captured, being sold.[14]

Outline

Construct an outline for an essay on the following question. What were the context, process, and impact of the conquests of Alexander the Great?

---

14 Arrian of Nicomedia. *The Anabasis of Alexander*, ebook. Translated by E. J. Chinnock. Project Gutenberg. https://www.gutenberg.org/files/46976/46976-h/46976-h.htm. (Accessed April 16, 2021).

Lesson 14

Hellenization and the Maccabees

Vocabulary

Define each term in 5 sentences.

Hellenistic Philosophy

Hellenistic Kingdoms

Maccabean Revolt

Quiz

From the Lecture

1. The word "cynic" is based on the Greek word for:
    - A. philosopher.
    - B. king.
    - C. dog.
    - D. skeptic.

2. What best describes Epicureans?
    - A. They seek a virtuous life.
    - B. They seek pleasure in a simple life.
    - C. They are hedonists.
    - D. They reject all truth.

3. Who proposed a heliocentric view of the solar system?
    - A. Euclid
    - B. Archimedes
    - C. Zeno
    - D. Aristarchus

4. Who seized control of Egypt after the death of Alexander?
    A. Ptolemy
    B. Selecucus
    C. Antigonus
    D. Perdiccas

5. What did Jason do in Jerusalem when he came to power as a high priest?
    A. rebuild the walls
    B. dedicate the temple to Zeus
    C. build a gymnasium
    D. kill Onias

6. One theory is that "Maccabee" was a personal title for Judas meaning:
    A. "hammer."
    B. "king."
    C. "warrior."
    D. "priest."

7. Which one of the following is not a son Mattathias?
    A. John
    B. Jonathan
    C. Eleazar
    D. David

8. The rededication of the temple under the Maccabees is remembered in what Jewish festival?
    A. Hanukkah
    B. Tabernacles
    C. Passover
    D. Rosh Hashana

9. How did Eleazar die?
    A. double-crossed by the Seleucid ruler
    B. crushed by an elephant
    C. killed by his son-in-law
    D. shot by an arrow

10. Who came to power after the death of the five Maccabee brothers?
    A. John Hyrcanus
    B. Judah Aristobulus I
    C. Antigonus I
    D. Alexander Jannai

Writing Assignment

Read the following excerpt from 1 Maccabees. Write a short 300-word essay answering the following question. What did King Antiochus require of the Jews and what was the reaction of Mattathias?

1 Maccabees 2:6–30

6 These saw the evils that were done in the people of Juda, and in Jerusalem. 7 And Mathathias said: Woe is me, wherefore was I born to see the ruin of my people, and the ruin of the holy city, and to dwell there, when it is given into the hands of the enemies? 8 The holy places are come into the hands of strangers: her temple is become as a man without honour. 9 The vessels of her glory are carried away captive: her old men are murdered in the streets, and her young men are fallen by the sword of the enemies. 10 What nation hath not inherited her kingdom, and gotten of her spoils?

11 All her ornaments are taken away. She that was free is made a slave. 12 And behold our sanctuary, and our beauty, and our glory is laid waste, and the Gentiles have defiled them. 13 To what end then should we live any longer? 14 And Mathathias and his sons rent their garments, and they covered themselves with haircloth, and made great lamentation. 15 And they that were sent from king Antiochus came thither, to compel them that were fled into the city of Modin, to sacrifice, and to burn incense, and to depart from the law of God.

16 And many of the people of Israel consented, and came to them: but Mathathias and his sons stood firm. 17 And they that were sent from Antiochus, answering, said to Mathathias: Thou art a ruler, and an honourable, and great man in this city, and adorned with sons, and brethren. 18 Therefore come thou first, and obey the king's commandment, as all nations have done, and the men of Juda, and they that remain in Jerusalem: and thou, and thy sons, shall be in the number of the king's friends, and enriched with gold, and silver, and many presents. 19 Then Mathathias answered, and said with a loud voice: Although all nations obey king Antiochus, so as to depart every man from the service of the law of his fathers, and consent to his commandments: 20 I and my sons, and my brethren will obey the law of our fathers.

21 God be merciful unto us: it is not profitable for us to forsake the law, and the justices of God: 22 We will not hearken to the words of king Antiochus, neither will we sacrifice, and transgress the commandments of our law, to go another way. 23 Now as he left off speaking these words, there came a certain Jew in the sight of all to sacrifice to the idols upon the altar in the city of Modin, according to the king's commandment. 24 And Mathathias saw and was grieved, and his reins trembled, and his wrath was kindled according to the judgment of the law, and running upon him he slew him upon the altar: 25 Moreover the man whom king Antiochus had sent, who compelled them to sacrifice, he slew at the same time, and pulled down the altar.

26 And shewed zeal for the law, as Phinees did by Zamri the son of Salomi. 27 And Mathathias cried out in the city with a loud voice, saying: Every one that hath zeal for the law, and maintaineth the testament, let him follow me. 28 So he, and his sons fled into the mountains, and left all that they had in the city. 29 Then many that sought after judgment, and justice, went down into the desert: 30 And they abode there, they and their children, and their wives, and their cattle: because afflictions increased upon them.[15]

---

15 *Douay-Rheims Bible,* website. Edited by Richard Challoner. Drbo.org. http://www.drbo.org/chapter/45002.htm. Accessed February 4, 2021.

Outline

Construct an outline for an essay on the following question. What was Hellenization and what was its impact on philosophy, politics, and religion (Maccabean revolt)?

Lesson 15

The Midterm

Study Guide

Identifications (100 points)

State what/who, when, where, and significance of the following terms in five sentences for each term. Eight terms will be presented to you on the exam, and you will have to do five. Use the vocabulary assignments to help study.

1. Ancient History
2. Christendom
3. Western Civilization
4. Agricultural (Neolithic) Revolution
5. Characteristics of a Civilization
6. Ancient Mesopotamia
7. Nile River
8. Pharaoh
9. Indus River Valley Civilization
10. The Bible as a historical document
11. Abraham
12. Jacob (Israel)
13. The Exodus
14. Moses
15. Mosaic Law
16. Joshua
17. Era of the Judges
18. David
19. Hittites
20. Phoenicians
21. Assyrians
22. Kingdom of Israel
23. Kingdom of Judah
24. Prophets (Isaiah and Jeremiah)

25. Nebuchadnezzar II
26. Cyrus the Great
27. Persian Empire
28. Minoans
29. Mycenaeans
30. Homer
31. Sparta
32. Athens
33. Persian Wars
34. Greek Philosophers
35. Greek Historians
36. Greek Tragedies
37. Philip II of Macedon
38. Alexander the Great
39. Alexander's Conquest of Persia
40. Hellenistic Philosophy
41. Hellenistic Kingdoms
42. Maccabean Revolt

Essays (100 Points)

In several short paragraphs, answer the following questions. Four questions will be presented to you, and you will have to do two. Use the outline assignment to help study.

1. What is history? How are ancient history, Christendom, and Western Civilization similar and different?

2. What is a civilization? What are the main characteristics of Ancient Mesopotamia?

3. What was the role of geography in ancient history? What were the main characteristics of Ancient Egypt and Ancient India (Indus River Valley and Vedic Period)?

4. Why can the Bible be used as a historical source? What was the historical significance of Abraham, Isaac, and Jacob (Israel)?

5. What was the role of the exodus and Moses in Ancient Israel?

6. How did the Israelites conquer the Promised Land and establish a kingdom?

7. How did the Hittites, Phoenicians, and Assyrians expand, and what were some characteristics of their states?

8. What were the events that led to the division of the kingdom? What were the main characteristics of the Kingdom of Israel and the Kingdom of Judah?

9. What were the differences and similarities between the Neo-Babylonians and Persians with particular attention given to the monarchs and treatment of the Jews?
10. What were the Minoan, Mycenaean, and literary roots (Homer) of Greek civilization?
11. What were the political systems of Athens and Sparta? What were the main characteristics of the Greco-Persian Wars and the Peloponnesian War?
12. What are the contributions of Ancient Greece in philosophy, history, and the arts?
13. What were the context, process, and impact of the conquests of Alexander the Great?
14. What was Hellenization and what was its impact on philosophy, politics, and religion (Maccabean revolt)?

Midterm Exam

A parent should randomly select eight terms from the identification section and four questions from the essay section. The selections should be balanced and from different lessons. For example, there should not be two terms from the same lesson, such as "Nile River" and "Pharoah," and there also should not be a term and an essay question from the same lesson, such as "Myceneans" as a term and "What were the Minoan, Mycenaean, and literary roots (Homer) of Greek civilization?" as an essay question. A sample exam is below. Students should have a finite time to complete the exam (two hours is suggested), and they should not have access to notes, the textbook, or the internet.

Sample Midterm

Identifications (100 points)

State what/who, when, where and significance of five and only five of the following terms in five sentences for each term.

1. Pharaoh
2. Abraham
3. Era of the Judges
4. Assyrians
5. Cyrus the Great
6. Greek Philosophers
7. Philip II of Macedon
8. Maccabean Revolt

Essays (100 Points)

In several short paragraphs, answer two and only two of following questions. Each of the two essays should have an introduction, several body paragraphs, and a conclusion.

1. What is a civilization? What are the main characteristics of Ancient Mesopotamia?

2. What was the role of the exodus and Moses in Ancient Israel?

3. What were the events that led to the division of the kingdom? What were the main characteristics of the Kingdom of Israel and the Kingdom of Judah?

4. What were the political systems of Athens and Sparta? What were the main characteristics of the Greco-Persian Wars and the Peloponnesian War?

Grading the Midterm

The exams are worth 200 points. Each of the five terms is worth 20 points for a total of 100 points and each of the two essays is worth 50 points for a total of 100 points. The exams are based on the vocabulary and outline assignments, and the completed vocabulary and outlines assignments should be used as a guide to grade to the exam.

Lesson 16

Rome: A Military Power

Vocabulary

Define each term in 5 sentences.

Roman Conquest of Italy

Roman Legions

Punic War

Quiz

From the Lecture

1. What foreign power dominated Rome during the period of kings?
   - A. Carthaginians
   - B. Etruscans
   - C. Greeks
   - D. Celts

2. Who or what warned the Romans during the Celtic attack on Capitoline Hill?
   - A. dogs
   - B. guards
   - C. geese
   - D. spies

3. What was one reason for Roman success in the conquest of Italy?
   - A. They used the phalanx system.
   - B. They shifted to maniple units.
   - C. They acquired war elephants.
   - D. They controlled the seas.

4. What civic and religious ritual was held in Rome to celebrate a military victory?
   A. triumph
   B. sacrifice to Juno
   C. Olympic games
   D. senatorial banquet

5. What battle in North Africa determined the outcome of the Second Punic War?
   A. Mylae
   B. Aegates Sea
   C. Zama
   D. Cannae

From the Textbook

6. After the Celts sacked Rome, the city did not fall to another army until:
   A. 44 BC.
   B. AD 105.
   C. AD 303.
   D. AD 410.

7. What is a Pyrrhic victory?
   A. quick and easy
   B. too costly to bear
   C. won through treachery
   D. a defeat

8. In the First Punic War, Hannibal crossed the Alps to attack Rome.
   A. True
   B. False

9. What battle was the greatest victory for Hannibal and the worst defeat for Rome during the Punic Wars?
   A. Mylae
   B. Sicily
   C. Zama
   D. Cannae

10. What power employed Hannibal to form a navy in its fight against Rome?
   A. Seleucid
   B. Epirus
   C. Corinth
   D. Macedon

Writing Assignment

Read the following excerpt from Livy's *The History of Rome*. Write a short 300-word essay answering the following questions. Why did the Carthaginians (with the Gauls and Spaniards) win the Battle of Cannae? What does the actions of Paulus tell us about the character of the Roman soldier?

The History of Rome, Book 22

Chapter 47

When the battle shout was raised the auxiliaries ran forward, and the battle began with the light infantry. Then the Gauls and Spaniards on the left engaged the Roman cavalry on the right; the battle was not at all like a cavalry fight, for there was no room for maneuvering, the river on the one side and the infantry on the other hemming them in, compelled them to fight face to face. Each side tried to force their way straight forward, till at last the horses were standing in a closely pressed mass, and the riders seized their opponents and tried to drag them from their horses. It had become mainly a struggle of infantry, fierce but short, and the Roman cavalry was repulsed and fled. Just as this battle of the cavalry was finished, the infantry became engaged, and as long as the Gauls and Spaniards kept their ranks unbroken, both sides were equally matched in strength and courage. At length after long and repeated efforts the Romans closed up their ranks, echeloned their front, and by the sheer weight of their deep column bore down the division of the enemy which was stationed in front of Hannibal's line, and was too thin and weak to resist the pressure. Without a moment's pause they followed up their broken and hastily retreating foe till they took to headlong flight. Cutting their way through the mass of fugitives, who offered no resistance, they penetrated as far as the Africans who were stationed on both wings, somewhat further back than the Gauls and Spaniards who had formed the advanced centre. As the latter fell back the whole front became level, and as they continued to give ground it became concave and crescent-shaped, the Africans at either end forming the horns. As the Romans rushed on incautiously between them, they were enfiladed by the two wings, which extended and closed round them in the rear. On this, the Romans, who had fought one battle to no purpose, left the Gauls and Spaniards, whose rear they had been slaughtering, and commenced a fresh struggle with the Africans. The contest was a very one-sided one, for not only were they hemmed in on all sides, but wearied with the previous fighting they were meeting fresh and vigorous opponents.

Chapter 48

By this time the Roman left wing, where the allied cavalry were fronting the Numidians, had become engaged, but the fighting was slack at first owing to a Carthaginian stratagem. About 500 Numidians, carrying, besides their usual arms and missiles, swords concealed under their coats of mail, rode out from their own line with their shields slung behind their backs as though they were deserters, and suddenly leaped from their horses and flung their shields and javelins at the feet of their enemy. They were received into their ranks, conducted to the rear, and ordered to remain quiet. While the battle was spreading to the various parts of the field they remained quiet, but when the eyes and minds of all were wholly taken up with the fighting they seized the large Roman shields which were lying everywhere amongst the heaps of slain and commenced a furious attack upon the rear of the Roman line.

Slashing away at backs and hips, they made a great slaughter and a still greater panic and confusion. Amidst the rout and panic in one part of the field and the obstinate but hopeless struggle in the other, Hasdrubal, who was in command of that arm, withdrew some Numidians from the centre of the right wing, where the fighting was feebly kept up, and sent them m pursuit of the fugitives, and at the same time sent the Spanish and Gaulish horse to the aid of the Africans, who were by this time more wearied by slaughter than by fighting.

Chapter 49

Paulus was on the other side of the field. In spite of his having been seriously wounded at the commencement of the action by a bullet from a sling, he frequently encountered Hannibal with a compact body of troops, and in several places restored the battle. The Roman cavalry formed a bodyguard round him, but at last, as he became too weak to manage his horse, they all dismounted. It is stated that when some one reported to Hannibal that the consul had ordered his men to fight on foot, he remarked, "I would rather he handed them over to me bound hand and foot." Now that the victory of the enemy was no longer doubtful this struggle of the dismounted cavalry was such as might be expected when men preferred to die where they stood rather than flee, and the victors, furious at them for delaying the victory, butchered without mercy those whom they could not dislodge. They did, however, repulse a few survivors exhausted with their exertions and their wounds. All were at last scattered, and those who could regained their horses for flight. Cn. Lentulus, a military tribune, saw, as he rode by, the consul covered with blood sitting on a boulder. "Lucius Aemilius," he said, "the one man whom the gods must hold guiltless of this day's disaster, take this horse while you have still some strength left, and I can lift you into the saddle and keep by your side to protect you. Do not make this day of battle still more fatal by a consul's death, there are enough tears and mourning without that." The consul replied: "Long may you live to do brave deeds, Cornelius, but do not waste in useless pity the few moments left in which to escape from the hands of the enemy. Go, announce publicly to the senate that they must fortify Rome and make its defence strong before the victorious enemy approaches, and tell Q. Fabius privately that I have ever remembered his precepts in life and in death. Suffer me to breathe my last among my slaughtered soldiers, let me not have to defend myself again when I am no longer consul, or appear as the accuser of my colleague and protect my own innocence by throwing the guilt on another." During this conversation a crowd of fugitives came suddenly upon them, followed by the enemy, who, not knowing who the consul was, overwhelmed him with a shower of missiles. Lentulus escaped on horseback in the rush.[16]

Outline

Construct an outline for an essay on the following questions. How did Rome conquer the Mediterranean world? Why was their military so successful?

16 Titus Livius. *The History of Rome, ebook.* Translated by Rev. Canon Roberts. Wikisource. https://en.wikisource.org/wiki/From_the_Founding_of_the_City/Book_22#45. Accessed April 28, 2021.

Lesson 17

Roman Republic

Vocabulary

Define each term in 5 sentences.

Kings of Rome

Magistrates of Rome

Patricians and Plebeians

Quiz

From the Lecture

1. According to tradition, when was Rome founded by Romulus?
    - A. 509 BC
    - B. 753 BC
    - C. 909 BC
    - D. 1023 BC

2. There were how many legendary kings of Rome?
    - A. 4
    - B. 6
    - C. 7
    - D. 9

3. What was the pivotal event that led to the end of the Roman Kingdom?
    - A. sack of Rome
    - B. the great drought
    - C. defeat at Veii
    - D. rape of Lucretia

4. What best describes the senate?
   A. They had limited real powers in the Roman constitution.
   B. They elected magistrates.
   C. They lead armies into battle.
   D. They represented the plebs.

5. Which of the Roman assemblies was originally tied to the military?
   A. Comitia Centuriata
   B. Comitia Curiata
   C. Comitia Tributa

6. The plebeians could challenge the power of the patricians through all the following ways EXCEPT:
   A. the concilium plebis.
   B. the tribunes.
   C. service in the military.
   D. the senate.

From the Textbook

7. What Roman magistrate was elected every five years?
   A. censor
   B. quaestor
   C. praetor
   D. consul

8. How were consuls selected?
   A. by the senate
   B. by the comitia centuriata
   C. by the king
   D. by the tribes

9. What magistrate carried out judicial duties?
   A. censor
   B. quaestor
   C. praetor
   D. consul

10. All the following statements about tribunes are true EXCEPT:
   A. They had to be a patrician.
   B. They were elected by the concilium plebis.
   C. They could veto bills.
   D. Anyone harming them could be killed without a trial.

Writing Assignment

Read the following excerpt from Polybius's *The Histories*. Write a short 300-word essay answering the following question. How was the Roman constitution balanced between three different elements?

Volume 1: Book VI, Chapters 11–14

11. As for the Roman constitution, it had three elements, each of them possessing sovereign powers: and their respective share of power in the whole state had been regulated with such a scrupulous regard to equality and equilibrium, that no one could say for certain, not even a native, whether the constitution as a whole were an aristocracy or democracy or despotism. And no wonder: for if we confine our observation to the power of the Consuls we should be inclined to regard it as despotic; if on that of the Senate, as aristocratic; and if finally one looks at the power possessed by the people it would seem a clear case of a democracy. What the exact powers of these several parts were, and still, with slight modifications, are, I will now state.

12. The Consuls, before leading out the legions, remain in Rome and are supreme masters of the administration. All other magistrates, except the Tribunes, are under them and take their orders. They introduce foreign ambassadors to the Senate; bring matters requiring deliberation before it; and see to the execution of its decrees. If, again, there are any matters of state which require the authorization of the people, it is their business to see to them, to summon the popular meetings, to bring the proposals before them, and to carry out the decrees of the majority. In the preparations for war also, and in a word in the entire administration of a campaign, they have all but absolute power. It is competent to them to impose on the allies such levies as they think good, to appoint the Military Tribunes, to make up the roll for soldiers and select those that are suitable. Besides they have absolute power of inflicting punishment on all who are under their command while on active service and they have authority to expend as much of the public money as they choose, being accompanied by a quaestor who is entirely at their orders. A survey of these powers would in fact justify our describing the constitution as despotic,—a clear case of royal government. Nor will it affect the truth of my description, if any of the institutions I have described are changed in our time, or in that of our posterity: and the same remarks apply to what follows.

13. The Senate has first of all the control of the treasury, and regulates the receipts and disbursements alike. For the Quaestors cannot issue any public money for the various departments of the state without a decree of the Senate, except for the service of the Consuls. The Senate controls also what is by far the largest and most important expenditure, that, namely, which is made by the censors every lustrum for the repair or construction of public buildings; this money cannot be obtained by the censors except by the grant of the Senate. Similarly all crimes committed in Italy requiring a public investigation, such as treason, conspiracy, poisoning, or wilful murder, are in the hands of the Senate. Besides, if any individual or state among the Italian allies requires a controversy to be settled, a penalty to be assessed, help or protection to be afforded,—all this is the province of the Senate. Or again, outside Italy, if it is necessary to send an embassy to reconcile warring communities, or to remind them of their duty, or sometimes to impose requisitions upon them, or to receive their submission, or finally to proclaim war against them,—this too is the business of the Senate. In like manner the reception to be given to foreign ambassadors in Rome, and the answers to be returned to

them, are decided by the Senate. With such business the people have nothing to do. Consequently, if one were staying at Rome when the Consuls were not in town, one would imagine the constitution to be a complete aristocracy: and this has been the idea entertained by many Greeks, and by many kings as well, from the fact that nearly all the business they had with Rome was settled by the Senate.

14. After this one would naturally be inclined to ask what part is left for the people in the constitution, when the Senate has these various functions, especially the control of the receipts and expenditure of the exchequer; and when the Consuls, again, have absolute power over the details of military preparation, and an absolute authority in the field? There is, however, a part left the people, and it is a most important one. For the people is the sole fountain of honour and of punishment; and it is by these two things and these alone that dynasties and constitutions and, in a word, human society are held together: for where the distinction between them is not sharply drawn both in theory and practice, there no undertaking can be properly administered,—as indeed we might expect when good and bad are held in exactly the same honour. The people then are the only court to decide matters of life and death; and even in cases where the penalty is money, if the sum to be assessed is sufficiently serious, and especially when the accused have held the higher magistracies. And in regard to this arrangement there is one point deserving especial commendation and record. Men who are on trial for their lives at Rome, while sentence is in process of being voted,—if even only one of the tribes whose votes are needed to ratify the sentence has not voted,—have the privilege at Rome of openly departing and condemning themselves to a voluntary exile. Such men are safe at Naples or Praeneste or at Tibur, and at other towns with which this arrangement has been duly ratified on oath. Again, it is the people who bestow offices on the deserving, which are the most honourable rewards of virtue. It has also the absolute power of passing or repealing laws; and, most important of all, it is the people who deliberate on the question of peace or war. And when provisional terms are made for alliance, suspension of hostilities, or treaties, it is the people who ratify them or the reverse. These considerations again would lead one to say that the chief power in the state was the people's, and that the constitution was a democracy.[17]

Outline

Construct an outline for an essay on the following questions. How did Rome transition from a kingdom to a republic? What were the main political features of the Roman Republic?

17 Polybius. *The Histories of Polybius, Vol. I, ebook.* Translated by Evelyn Shirley Shuckburgh. Guteburg Project. https://www.gutenberg.org/files/44125/44125-h/44125-h.htm. Accessed May 11, 2021.

Lesson 18

Era of Roman Civil Wars

Vocabulary

Define each term in 5 sentences.

Optimates and Populares

Soldier-Heroes (Marius, Sulla, Pompey)

Julius Caesar

Quiz

From the Lecture

1. What was the main source of tension in second-century (BC) Italy?
    - A. military defeats
    - B. uneven land distribution
    - C. shortage of women
    - D. tyrant kings

2. What position did Sulla assume after his final defeat of the populares?
    - A. consul
    - B. king
    - C. dictator
    - D. censor

3. Who was NOT a member of the first triumvirate?
    - A. Pompey
    - B. Caesar
    - C. Crassus
    - D. Cicero

4. What was Julius Caesar's most significant conquest?
    A. Gaul
    B. England
    C. Egypt
    D. Sicily

5. What group was responsible for the assassination of Julius Caesar?
    A. populares
    B. Egyptians
    C. Greeks
    D. senators

From the Textbook

6. How many followers of Gaius Gracchus were killed with him?
    A. 100
    B. 300
    C. 2,000
    D. 3,000

7. The optimates represented the poor of Rome.
    A. True
    B. False

8. What was the cause of the Social War?
    A. the Italian allies' desire for citizenship and the right to vote
    B. the struggle between the populares and optimates in Rome
    C. an invasion of Germans in the north
    D. a slave revolt in Sicily

9. In Ancient Rome, what did it mean to be proscribed?
    A. elected by popular vote
    B. given a triumph
    C. put on a list to be killed
    D. made a gladiator

10. Caesar is alleged to have said "The die is cast" in reference to what action?
    A. crossing the Rubicon River
    B. killing Pompey
    C. forming the First Triumvirate
    D. defeating the Gauls

Writing Assignment

Read the following excerpt from Plutarch's *Life of Caesar*. Write a short 300-word essay answering the following question. Why did Caesar's men love and respect him?

Volume III

XVI. So great were the good-will and devotion of Caesar's soldiers to him, that those who under other generals were in no way superior to ordinary soldiers, were invincible and irresistible and ready to meet any danger for Caesar's glory. An instance of this is Acilius, who in the sea-fight of Massalia boarded one of the enemy's ships and had his right hand cut off with a sword, but he still kept hold of his shield with the left hand and striking at the faces of the enemy drove all to flight and got possession of the vessel. Another instance was Cassius Scaeva, who in the fight at Dyrrachium had one eye destroyed by an arrow, his shoulder transfixed with one javelin and his thigh with another, and on his shield he had received the blows of one hundred and thirty missiles. In this plight he called to the enemy as if he designed to surrender himself, and two of them accordingly approached him, but with his sword he lopped off one man's shoulder and wounding the other in the face, put him to flight, and finally he escaped himself with the aid of his friends. In Britannia on one occasion the natives had attacked the foremost centurions who had got into a marshy spot full of water, upon which, in the presence of Caesar who was viewing the contest, a soldier rushed into the midst of the enemy, and after performing many conspicuous acts of valor, rescued the centurions from the barbarians, who took to flight. The soldier, with difficulty attempting to cross after all the rest, plunged into the muddy stream, and with great trouble and the loss of his shield, sometimes swimming, sometimes walking, he got safe over. While those who were about Caesar were admiring his conduct and coming to receive him with congratulations and shouts, the soldier, with the greatest marks of dejection and tears in his eyes, fell down at Caesar's feet and begged pardon for the loss of his shield. Again, in Libya, Scipio's party having taken one of Caesar's ships in which was Granius Petro, who had been appointed quaestor, made booty of all the rest, but offered to give the quaestor his life; but he replying that it was the fashion with Caesar's soldiers to give and not to accept mercy, killed himself with his own sword.

XVII. This courage and emulation Caesar cherished and created, in the first place by distributing rewards and honors without stint, and thus showing that he did not get wealth from the enemy for his own enjoyment and pleasure, but that it was treasured up with him as the common reward of courage, and that he was rich only in proportion as he rewarded deserving soldiers; and in the next place by readily undergoing every danger and never shrinking from any toil. Now they did not so much admire Caesar's courage, knowing his love of glory; but his endurance of labor beyond his body's apparent power of sustaining it, was a matter of astonishment, for he was of a spare habit, and had a white and soft skin, and was subject to complaints in the head and to epileptic fits, which, as it is said, first attacked him at Corduba; notwithstanding all this, he did not make his feeble health an excuse for indulgence, but he made military service the means of his cure, by unwearied journeying, frugal diet, and by constantly keeping in the open air and enduring fatigue, struggling with his malady and keeping his body proof against its attacks. He generally slept in chariots or in litters, making even his repose a kind of action; and in the daytime he used to ride in a vehicle to the garrisons, cities and camps, with a slave by his side, one of those who were expert at taking down what was dictated on a journey, and a single soldier behind him armed with a sword. He used to travel so quick that on his first journey from Rome he reached the Rhodanus in eight days. From his boyhood he was a good horseman, for he had been accustomed to place his hands behind him and, holding them close together on his back, to put the horse to his full speed. In that campaign he also practiced himself in dictating letters as he was riding and thus giving employment to two scribes, and as Oppius says, to more. He is said also to have introduced the practice of communicating with his friends by letters, as there was no time for personal interviews on urgent affairs, owing to the amount of business and the size of the city. This anecdote also is cited as a proof of his indifference as to diet. On one occasion when he was entertained at supper by his host Valerius Leo in Mediolanum, asparagus was served up with myrum poured on it instead of oil, which Caesar ate without taking any notice of it, and reproved his friends who were out of humor on the occasion. "You should be content," he said, "not to eat what you don't like; but to find fault with your host's ill-breeding is to be as ill-bred as himself." Once upon a journey he was compelled by a storm to take shelter in a poor man's hut, which contained only a single chamber and that hardly large enough for one person, on which he observed to his friends that the post of honor must be given to the worthiest and the place of safety to the weakest; and he bade Oppius lie down while he and the rest slept in the porch.[18]

Outline

Construct an outline for an essay on the following question. What were the main divisions and hostilities during the civil wars at the end of the Roman Republic?

18 Plutarch. *Plutarch's Lives, Volume 3, ebook.* Translated by George Long. Gutenberg Project. https://www.gutenberg.org/files/14140/14140-h/14140-h.htm#LIFE_OF_C_CAESAR. Accessed May 11, 2021.

Lesson 19

Roman Culture

Vocabulary

Define each term in 5 sentences.

Roman Heroes

Roman Families

Roman Religion

Quiz

From the Lecture

1. Romans saw the Greeks as all the following EXCEPT:
    - A. feminine.
    - B. weak.
    - C. chaotic.
    - D. practical.

2. Which of the following was NOT a Roman historian?
    - A. Sallust
    - B. Cato
    - C. Tacitus
    - D. Suetonius

3. Cato the Elder can best be described as a:
    - A. Cynic.
    - B. Stoic.
    - C. Epicurean.
    - D. Skeptic.

4. Who was acclaimed as the greatest Roman orator?
    A. Sallust
    B. Lucretius
    C. Cicero
    D. Catullus

5. In Virgil's *Aeneid,* Aeneas was a refugee from what city?
    A. Troy
    B. Athens
    C. Jerusalem
    D. Tyre

6. In the Roman marriage ritual, the tradition to carry the bride over the threshold commemorates what event?
    A. the entrance of the Vestal Virgins
    B. the rites of Janus
    C. the abduction of the Sabine women
    D. a military triumph

7. Roman males typically had two names.
    A. True
    B. False

8. Young Roman males began their education at a Grammaticus.
    A. True
    B. False

9. In Roman mythology, who was considered king of the gods?
    A. Jupiter
    B. Zeus
    C. Juno
    D. Pluto

10. What was the Roman title for the chief priest?
    A. augers
    B. college of pontiffs
    C. pontifex maximus
    D. paterfamilias

Writing Assignment

Read the following excerpt from Livy's *The History of Rome.* Write a short 300-word essay answering the following question. What was the Roman view of women?

The History of Rome, Book 1, Chapter 9

And now the Roman state was become so powerful, that it was a match for any of the neighboring nations in war, but, from the paucity of women, its greatness could only last for one age of man; for they had no hope of issue at home, nor had they any intermarriages with their neighbors. Therefore, by the advice of the Fathers, Romulus sent ambassadors to the neighboring states to solicit an alliance and the privilege of intermarriage for his new subjects. "That cities, like every thing else, rose from very humble beginnings. That those which the gods and their own merit aided, gained great power and high renown. That he knew full well, both that the gods had aided the origin of Rome, and that merit would not be wanting. Wherefore that, as men, they should feel no reluctance to mix their blood and race with men." No where did the embassy obtain a favorable hearing: so much did they at the same time despise, and dread for themselves and their posterity, so great a power growing up in the midst of them. They were dismissed by the greater part with the repeated question, "Whether they had opened any asylum for women also, for that such a plan only could obtain them suitable matches?" The Roman youth resented this conduct bitterly, and the matter unquestionably began to point towards violence. Romulus, in order that he might afford a favorable time and place for this, dissembling his resentment, purposely prepares games in honor of Neptunus Equestris; he calls them Consualia. He then orders the spectacle to be proclaimed among their neighbors; and they prepare for the celebration with all the magnificence they were then acquainted with, or were capable of doing, that they might render the matter famous, and an object of expectation. Great numbers assembled, from a desire also of seeing the new city; especially their nearest neighbors, the Cæninenses, Crustumini, and Antemnates. Moreover the whole multitude of the Sabines came, with their wives and children. Having been hospitably invited to the different houses, when they had seen the situation, and fortifications, and the city crowded with houses, they became astonished that the Roman power had increased so rapidly. When the time of the spectacle came on, and while their minds and eyes were intent upon it, according to concert a tumult began, and upon a signal given the Roman youth ran different ways to carry off the virgins by force. A great number were carried off at hap-hazard, according as they fell into their hands. Persons from the common people, who had been charged with the task, conveyed to their houses some women of surpassing beauty, destined for the leading senators. They say that one, far distinguished beyond the others for stature and beauty, was carried off by the party of one Thalassius, and whilst many inquired to whom they were carrying her, they cried out every now and then, in order that no one might molest her, that she was being taken to Thalassius; that from this circumstance this term became a nuptial one. The festival being disturbed by this alarm, the parents of the young women retire in grief, appealing to the compact of violated hospitality, and invoking the god, to whose festival and games they had come, deceived by the pretence of religion and good faith. Neither had the ravished virgins better hopes of their condition, or less indignation. But Romulus in person went about and declared, "That what was done was owing to the pride of their fathers, who had refused to grant the privilege of marriage to their neighbors; but notwithstanding, they should be joined in lawful wedlock, participate in all their possessions and civil privileges, and, than which nothing can be dearer to the human heart, in their common children. He begged them only to assuage the fierceness of their anger, and cheerfully surrender their affections to those to whom fortune had consigned their persons."

The History of Rome, Book 1, Chapter 57

As it commonly happens in standing camps, the war being rather tedious than violent, furloughs were easily obtained, more so by the officers, however, than the common soldiers. The young princes sometimes spent their leisure hours in feasting and entertainments. One day as they were drinking in the tent of Sextus Tarquin, where Collatinus Tarquinius, the son of Egerius, was also at supper, mention was made of wives. Every one commended his own in an extravagant manner, till a dispute arising about it, Collatinus said, "There was no occasion for words, that it might be known in a few hours how far his Lucretia excelled all the rest. If then, added he, we have any share of the vigour of youth, let us mount our horses and examine the behaviour of our wives; that must be most satisfactory to every one, which shall meet his eyes on the unexpected arrival of the husband." They were heated with wine; "Come on, then," say all. They immediately galloped to Rome, where they arrived in the dusk of the evening. From thence they went to Collatia, where they find Lucretia, not like the king's daughters-in-law, whom they had seen spending their time in luxurious entertainments with their equals, but though at an advanced time of night, employed at her wool, sitting in the middle of the house amid her maids working around her. The merit of the contest regarding the ladies was assigned to Lucretia. Her husband on his arrival, and the Tarquinii, were kindly received; the husband, proud of his victory, gives the young princes a polite invitation. There the villanous passion for violating Lucretia by force seizes Sextus Tarquin; both her beauty, and her approved purity, act as incentives. And then, after this youthful frolic of the night, they return to the camp.[19]

Outline

Construct an outline for an essay on the following question. What were the key elements of Roman culture, including literature, history, families, and religion?

19 Titus Livius. *The History of Rome, Books 1 to 8, ebook*. Translated by D. Spillan. Project Gutenberg. http://www.gutenberg.org/files/19725/19725-h/19725-h.htm. Accessed on 4/27/2021.

Lesson 20

Augustus

Vocabulary

Define each term in 5 sentences.

Second Triumvirate

Octavian's Triumph over Antony

Augustus' Political Settlement

Quiz

From the Lecture

1. Who was NOT a member of the Second Triumvirate?
   - A. Cicero
   - B. Antony
   - C. Octavian
   - D. Lepidus

2. How many senators were put on a death list during the proscription of the Second Triumvirate?
   - A. 5
   - B. 10
   - C. 135
   - D. 300

3. How did Antony and Octavian strengthen their alliance?
   - A. Antony recognized Caesar's son with Cleopatra.
   - B. Antony moved to Egypt to control Cleopatra.
   - C. Antony married Octavian's sister.
   - D. Antony fought Octavian's enemies in Sicily.

4. What did the Egyptian fleet under Cleopatra do in the Battle of Actium?
   A. left without engaging the enemy
   B. captured Octavian's ship
   C. surrendered
   D. led Antony to victory

5. What marked the northern border of the Roman Empire in central Europe?
   A. North Sea
   B. Alps
   C. Danube River
   D. Caspian Sea

From the Textbook

6. How old was Octavian when Caesar was assassinated?
   A. 18
   B. 21
   C. 23
   D. 24

7. Who seized control of Sicily in his struggle against Octavian?
   A. Sextus Pompey
   B. Antony
   C. Lepidus
   D. Agrippa

8. What Roman ritual marks the beginning of a period of peace?
   A. a military triumph
   B. closing the gates to the Temple of Janus
   C. the lighting of the eternal flame in the Temple of Vesta
   D. the sacrifice of a lion

9. What title did Octavian take that means "first citizen"?
   A. Augustus
   B. Emperor
   C. Caesar
   D. Princeps

10. What did Herod do with the temple?
   A. destroyed the temple
   B. turned the temple in a pagan site
   C. rebuilt the temple as larger and taller than the original
   D. sold the temple to the Romans

Writing Assignment

Read the following excerpt from Augustus's *The Deeds of the Divine Augustus*. Write a short 300-word essay answering the following questions. What did Augustus see as his main accomplishments? What do these accomplishments tell us about his character?

The Deeds of the Divine Augustus

2. I drove the men who slaughtered my father into exile with a legal order, punishing their crime, and afterwards, when they waged war on the state, I conquered them in two battles.

3. I often waged war, civil and foreign, on the earth and sea, in the whole wide world, and as victor I spared all the citizens who sought pardon. As for foreign nations, those which I was able to safely forgive, I preferred to preserve than to destroy. About five hundred thousand Roman citizens were sworn to me. I led something more than three hundred thousand of them into colonies and I returned them to their cities, after their stipend had been earned, and I assigned all of them fields or gave them money for their military service. I captured six hundred ships in addition to those smaller than triremes.

4. Twice I triumphed with an ovation, and three times I enjoyed a curule triumph and twenty-one times I was named emperor. When the senate decreed more triumphs for me, I sat out from all of them. I placed the laurel from the fasces in the Capitol, when the vows which I pronounced in each war had been fulfilled. On account of the things successfully done by me and through my officers, under my auspices, on earth and sea, the senate decreed fifty-five times that there be sacrifices to the immortal gods. Moreover there were 890 days on which the senate decreed there would be sacrifices. In my triumphs kings and nine children of kings were led before my chariot. I had been consul thirteen times, when I wrote this, and I was in the thirty-seventh year of tribunician power [14 C.E.].

5. When the dictatorship was offered to me, both in my presence and my absence, by the people and senate, when Marcus Marcellus and Lucius Arruntius were consuls [22 BC] I did not accept it. I did not evade the curatorship of grain in the height of the food shortage, which I so arranged that within a few days I freed the entire city from the present fear and danger by my own expense and administration. When the annual and perpetual consulate was then again offered to me, I did not accept it.

6. When Marcus Vinicius and Quintus Lucretius were consuls [19 BC], then again when Publius Lentulus and Gnaeus Lentulus were [18 BC], and third when Paullus Fabius Maximus and Quintus Tubero were [11 BC], although the senate and Roman people consented that I alone be made curator of the laws and customs with the highest power, I received no magistracy offered contrary to the customs of the ancestors. What the senate then wanted to accomplish through me, I did through tribunician power, and five times on my own accord I both requested and received from the senate a colleague in such power.

13. Our ancestors wanted Janus Quirinus to be closed when throughout the all the rule of the Roman people, by land and sea, peace had been secured through victory. Although before my birth it had been closed twice in all in recorded memory from the founding of the city, the senate voted three times in my principate that it be closed.

15. I paid to the Roman plebs, HS 300 per man from my father's will and in my own name gave

HS 400 from the spoils of war when I was consul for the fifth time [29 BC]; furthermore I again paid out a public gift of HS 400 per man, in my tenth consulate [24 BC], from my own patrimony; and, when consul for the eleventh time [23 BC], twelve doles of grain personally bought were measured out; and in my twelfth year of tribunician power [12-11 BC] I gave HS 400 per man for the third time. And these public gifts of mine never reached fewer than 250,000 men. In my eighteenth year of tribunician power, as consul for the twelfth time [5 BC], I gave to 320,000 plebs of the city HS 240 per man. And, when consul the fifth time [29 BC], I gave from my war-spoils to colonies of my soldiers each HS 1000 per man; about 120,000 men in the colonies received this triumphal public gift. Consul for the thirteenth time [2 BC], I gave HS 240 to the plebs who then received the public grain; they were a few more than 200,000.

16. I paid the towns money for the fields which I had assigned to soldiers in my fourth consulate [30 BC] and then when Marcus Crassus and Gnaeus Lentulus Augur were consuls [14 BC]; the sum was about HS 600,000,000 which I paid out for Italian estates, and about HS 260,000,000 which I paid for provincial fields. I was first and alone who did this among all who founded military colonies in Italy or the provinces according to the memory of my age. And afterwards, when Tiberius Nero and Gnaeus Piso were consuls [7 BC and likewise when Gaius Antistius and Decius Laelius were consuls [6 BC.], and when Gaius Calvisius and Lucius Passienus were consuls [4 BC], and when Lucius Lentulus and Marcus Messalla were consuls [3 BC], and when Lucius Caninius and Quintus Fabricius were consuls [2 BC I paid out rewards in cash to the soldiers whom I had led into their towns when their service was completed, and in this venture I spent about HS 400,000,000.

18. From that year when Gnaeus and Publius Lentulus were consuls (18 BC), when the taxes fell short, I gave out contributions of grain and money from my granary and patrimony, sometimes to 100,000 men, sometimes to many more.

25. I restored peace to the sea from pirates. In that slave war I handed over to their masters for the infliction of punishments about 30,000 captured, who had fled their masters and taken up arms against the state. All Italy swore allegiance to me voluntarily, and demanded me as leader of the war which I won at Actium; the provinces of Gaul, Spain, Africa, Sicily, and Sardinia swore the same allegiance. And those who then fought under my standard were more than 700 senators, among whom 83 were made consuls either before or after, up to the day this was written, and about 170 were made priests.

26. I extended the borders of all the provinces of the Roman people which neighbored nations not subject to our rule. I restored peace to the provinces of Gaul and Spain, likewise Germany, which includes the ocean from Cadiz to the mouth of the river Elbe. I brought peace to the Alps from the region which is near the Adriatic Sea to the Tuscan, with no unjust war waged against any nation. I sailed my ships on the ocean from the mouth of the Rhine to the east region up to the borders of the Cimbri, where no Roman had gone before that time by land or sea, and the Cimbri and the Charydes and the Semnones and the other Germans of the same territory sought by envoys the friendship of me and of the Roman people. By my order and auspices two armies were led at about the same time into Ethiopia and into that part of Arabia which is called Happy, and the troops of each nation of enemies were slaughtered in battle and many towns captured. They penetrated into Ethiopia all the way

to the town Nabata, which is near to Meroe; and into Arabia all the way to the border of the Sabaei, advancing to the town Mariba.[20]

Outline

Construct an outline for an essay on the following questions. How did Augustus come to power? What political and military actions did he do when in power?

20 Augustus Caesar. Res Gestae Divi Augusti. Translated by Thomas Bushnell. Wikisource. https://en.wikisource.org/wiki/The_Deeds_of_the_Divine_Augustus. Accessed May 12, 2021.

Lesson 21

Roman Society

Vocabulary

Define each term in 5 sentences.

Roman Buildings

Roman Trade

Roman Slavery

Quiz

From the Lecture

1. Which one of the following was NOT an ingredient in Roman cement?
   - A. petroleum
   - B. aggregate, like stone
   - C. lime
   - D. volcanic ash

2. What was the political, economic, and religious center of Rome during the Republic?
   - A. the Vatican
   - B. the Roman Forum
   - C. Palatine Hill
   - D. Circus Maximus

3. Who built the massive palace on top of Palatine Hill?
   - A. Nero
   - B. Caesar
   - C. Hadrian
   - D. Domitian

4. Wealthy Romans lived in an insula, which is based on the Latin word for island.
    A. True
    B. False

5. What crop was not part of the Mediterranean Triad?
    A. tomatoes
    B. grain
    C. grapes
    D. olives

6. What was the name of the country estates owned by wealthy Romans?
    A. domus
    B. mici
    C. villa
    D. portus

7. The Roman Empire had about 50,000 miles of stone-paved roads.
    A. True
    B. False

8. What Chinese product was sought after by the Romans?
    A. tea
    B. ivory
    C. silk
    D. amber

9. What was the role of Spartacus as a slave before the revolt?
    A. gladiator
    B. house slave
    C. miner
    D. farm hand

10. All the following are ways for a slave to be freed in Ancient Rome EXCEPT:
    A. being born to slave parents.
    B. buying freedom.
    C. being freed by the master.
    D. being freed in the will of the master.

Writing Assignment

Read the following excerpt from Plutarch's *Life of Crassus*. Write a short 300-word essay answering the following question. How did Crassus defeat Spartacus?

Life of Crassus, Chapter X

The Senate, on receiving this news, angrily bade the consuls keep quiet, and they appointed Crassus to the command of the war, whose reputation and popularity induced many of the nobles to serve under him. Crassus took his station on the frontiers of Picenum, with the view of waiting for Spartacus, who was moving in that direction; and he sent Mummius, his legatus, at the head of two legions, to make a circuit, and with orders to follow the enemy, but not to engage with them, nor come to close quarters. But Mummius, as soon as he got what he thought a favorable opportunity, fought a battle, and was defeated; many of his men fell, and many, flying without their arms, made their escape. Crassus received Mummius himself roughly, and arming the soldiers again, he required of them security for their arms, that they would keep them; and five hundred, who had been the first to run, and had shown most cowardice, he distributed into fifty decades, and out of each decade he took one man, by lot, and put him to death; thus inflicting on the soldiers this ancient mode of punishment which had long fallen into disuse; for disgrace also is added to the manner of death, and many things horrible and dreadful to see accompany the punishment, in the presence of all the spectators. After inflicting this punishment, he made his men again face about and march against the enemy. Spartacus, however, avoided Crassus, and made his way through Lucania to the sea, and, falling in with some Cilician piratical vessels, in the Straits, he formed a design to seize Sicily, and by throwing two thousand men into the island, to kindle again the servile war there, the flames of which had not long since been quenched, and required only a few sparks to set it again in a blaze. . . .

Life of Crassus, Chapter XI

The men of Crassus endeavored to escape notice by covering their helmets; but, being seen by two women, who were sacrificing for the enemy, they would have been in danger, if Crassus had not quickly appeared, and fought a battle, the most severely contested of all in this war, in which he destroyed twelve thousand three hundred men, of whom he found only two wounded in the back: all the rest died in the ranks, fighting against the Romans. After the defeat of this body, Spartacus retired to the mountains of Petilia, followed by Quintius, one of the generals of Crassus, and Scrofas, his quæstor, who hung close on his rear. But, upon Spartacus facing about, the Romans were thrown into disorderly flight, and made their escape, after having with difficulty rescued their quæstor, who was wounded. This success was the ruin of Spartacus, in consequence of the self-confidence which it infused into the slaves: they would not now consent to avoid a battle, nor yet would they obey their commanders, whom they surrounded, with arms in their hands, on the march, and compelled to lead them back through Lucania against the Romans, wherein they did the very thing that Crassus desired; for it was reported that Pompeius was now approaching, and there were not a few who openly said that the victory in this war belonged to him; for he would fight as soon as he arrived, and put an end to the campaign. While Crassus, therefore, who was eager to decide the affair by a battle, and to fix his camp near the enemy, was engaged in digging his trenches, the slaves came up to them and attacked the men who were at work. As fresh men from both sides kept coming up to help their comrades, Spartacus, seeing that he must fight, arranged all his army in order of battle. When his horse was brought to him, he drew his sword and said, that if he won the battle he should have plenty of fine horses from the enemy, and if he was defeated he should not want one; upon which he killed his horse, and then he made his way towards Crassus himself, through many men, and inflicting many wounds; but he did not succeed in reaching Crassus, though he engaged with and killed two centurions. At last, after those about him had fled, he kept his ground, and, being surrounded by a great number, he fought till he was cut down. But, though Crassus had been successful, and had displayed the skill of a great general, and had exposed his person to danger, yet the credit of the victory did not escape being appropriated to Pompeius; for those who fled from the battle were destroyed by him, and Pompeius wrote to the Senate that Crassus had defeated the slaves in the open field, but he had cut up the war by the roots.[21]

Outline

Construct an outline for an essay on the following question. What were the key elements of Roman society, including buildings, slavery, and trade?

21 Plutarch. *Plutarch's Lives, Volume III, ebook.* Translated by George Long. Gutenberg Project. https://www.gutenberg.org/files/14140/14140-h/14140-h.htm#LIFE_OF_CRASSUS. (Accessed May 4, 2021.

Lesson 22

The Incarnation

Vocabulary

Define each term in 5 sentences.

The Gospels

Herodian Rulers

The Holy Family

Quiz

From the Lecture

1. Which one of the four Gospels is the most unique?
   - A. Matthew
   - B. Mark
   - C. Luke
   - D. John

2. Herod I did all the following EXCEPT:
   - A. rebuild the Second Temple.
   - B. kill his wife, Mariamne.
   - C. place Jesus on trial.
   - D. become client king of Judea with Roman support.

3. What best describes the Zealots?
   - A. Jewish fighters against Rome
   - B. legal scholars upholding the purity of the law
   - C. aristocratic leaders allied with Rome
   - D. hermits with extreme ascetical practices

4. After the death of Herod I, Galilee was ruled by:
   A. a Roman procurator.
   B. Herod Antipas.
   C. Herod Archelaus.
   D. Philip.

5. What is the traditional location of the visitation of Mary and Elizabeth?
   A. Tiberius
   B. Cana
   C. Ain Karem
   D. Nazareth

From the Textbook

6. St. Peter was most likely a source for what Gospel?
   A. Matthew
   B. Mark
   C. Luke
   D. John

7. The earliest preserved fragment of the Gospel of John, the Ryland Papyrus, is dated to when?
   A. first century
   B. second century
   C. third century
   D. fourth century

8. What Romanized Jew provided another account of the life and death of Jesus?
   A. Tacitus
   B. Herod
   C. Josephus
   D. Thomas

9. In the meeting between Mary and Elizabeth, Mary's response is known as the:
   A. Hail Mary.
   B. Memorare.
   C. Hail Holy Queen.
   D. Magnificat.

10. According to the Gospel of Luke, who was the governor of Syria during the census around the time of the birth of Jesus?
    A. Pilate
    B. Quirinius
    C. Tiberius
    D. Caesar

Writing Assignment

Read the following excerpts from Flavius Josephus's *The Antiquities of the Jews* and Tacitus's *Annals*. Write a short 300-word essay answering the following questions. What do early non-Christian sources say about Jesus and his followers? What does it mean for the historical accuracy of the Gospels?

The Antiquities of the Jews, Book XVIII, Chapter 3

Now there was about this time Jesus, a wise man, if it be lawful to call him a man; for he was a doer of wonderful works, a teacher of such men as receive the truth with pleasure. He drew over to him both many of the Jews and many of the Gentiles. He was [the] Christ. And when Pilate, at the suggestion of the principal men amongst us, had condemned him to the cross, those that loved him at the first did not forsake him; for he appeared to them alive again the third day; as the divine prophets had foretold these and ten thousand other wonderful things concerning him. And the tribe of Christians, so named from him, are not extinct at this day.

Annals, Book XV, Chapter 44

But all human efforts, all the lavish gifts of the emperor, and the propitiations of the gods, did not banish the sinister belief that the conflagration was the result of an order. Consequently, to get rid of the report, Nero fastened the guilt and inflicted the most exquisite tortures on a class hated for their abominations, called Christians by the populace. Christus, from whom the name had its origin, suffered the extreme penalty during the reign of Tiberius at the hands of one of our procurators, Pontius Pilatus, and a most mischievous superstition, thus checked for the moment, again broke out not only in Judaea, the first source of the evil, but even in Rome, where all things hideous and shameful from every part of the world find their centre and become popular. Accordingly, an arrest was first made of all who pleaded guilty; then, upon their information, an immense multitude was convicted, not so much of the crime of firing the city, as of hatred against mankind. Mockery of every sort was added to their deaths. Covered with the skins of beasts, they were torn by dogs and perished, or were nailed to crosses, or were doomed to the flames and burnt, to serve as a nightly illumination, when daylight had expired. Nero offered his gardens for the spectacle, and was exhibiting a show in the circus, while he mingled with the people in the dress of a charioteer or stood aloft on a car. Hence, even for criminals who deserved extreme and exemplary punishment, there arose a feeling of compassion; for it was not, as it seemed, for the public good, but to glut one man's cruelty, that they were being destroyed.[22]

Outline

Construct an outline for an essay on the following questions. What are the historical sources for Jesus? What was the historical context (Jewish and Roman) at the time of his birth?

---

22 Flavius Josephus. *The Antiquities of the Jews, ebook.* Translated by William Whiston. Wikisource. https://en.wikisource.org/wiki/The_Antiquities_of_the_Jews/Book_XVIII#Chapter_3. Accessed April 20, 2021. Tacitus. *Annals, ebook.* Translated by Alfred John Church and William Jackson Brodribb. Wikisource. https://en.wikisource.org/wiki/The_Annals_(Tacitus)/Book_15#44. Accessed April 20, 2021.

Lesson 23

The Public Life, Death, and Resurrection of Jesus

Vocabulary

Define each term in 5 sentences.

Public Ministry of Jesus

Passion and Death of Jesus

Jesus: Resurrection to Ascension

Quiz

From the Lecture

1. Who was the emperor of Rome when Jesus began his public ministry?
    - A. Tiberius
    - B. Caesar
    - C. Augustus
    - D. Nero

2. The apostles St. Andrew and St. James the Greater were brothers.
    - A. True
    - B. False

3. Who was the only apostle not from Galilee
    - A. St. Simon
    - B. St. John
    - C. St. Thomas
    - D. Judas

4. What was NOT stated about St. Mary Magdalen in the Bible?
   A. She was a prostitute.
   B. She was at the crucifixion of Jesus.
   C. She was possessed by seven demons.
   D. She saw Jesus after the resurrection.

5. Who did not question Jesus during his passion?
   A. Pilate
   B. Caiaphas
   C. Herod Archelaus
   D. Annas

6. Of whom was it said "born of women there has risen not one greater"?
   A. St. Joseph
   B. St. Peter
   C. Moses
   D. St. John the Baptist

7. What town did Jesus use as his base in Galilee?
   A. Cana
   B. Bethany
   C. Capernaum
   D. Jericho

8. What was the 71-member ruling body of Judaism during the time of Jesus?
   A. Pharisee
   B. Sadducee
   C. High Priest
   D. Sanhedrin

9. What day is the feast of Passover?
   A. March 25
   B. 15 day of Nisan
   C. 25 day of Kislev
   D. April 1

10. About how far is the tomb of Jesus from the site of the crucifixion?
   A. 5 miles
   B. 1.2 miles
   C. 115 yards
   D. 22 yards

Writings Assignment

Read the following excerpt from the Gospel of Matthew. Write a short 300-word essay answering the following questions. What were the core teachings of Jesus? How were they different from the Greek and Roman worldview?

Matthew 5

1 And seeing the multitudes, he went up into a mountain, and when he was set down, his disciples
came unto him. 2 And opening his mouth, he taught them, saying: 3 Blessed are the poor in spirit:
for theirs is the kingdom of heaven. 4 Blessed are the meek: for they shall possess the land. 5 Blessed
are they that mourn: for they shall be comforted.

6 Blessed are they that hunger and thirst after justice: for they shall have their fill. 7 Blessed are
the merciful: for they shall obtain mercy. 8 Blessed are the clean of heart: for they shall see God. 9
Blessed are the peacemakers: for they shall be called children of God. 10 Blessed are they that suffer
persecution for justice' sake: for theirs is the kingdom of heaven.

11 Blessed are ye when they shall revile you, and persecute you, and speak all that is evil against
you, untruly, for my sake: 12 Be glad and rejoice, for your reward is very great in heaven. For so they
persecuted the prophets that were before you. 13 You are the salt of the earth. But if the salt lose
its savor, wherewith shall it be salted? It is good for nothing any more but to be cast out, and to be
trodden on by men. 14 You are the light of the world. A city seated on a mountain cannot be hid. 15
Neither do men light a candle and put it under a bushel, but upon a candlestick, that it may shine to
all that are in the house.

16 So let your light shine before men, that they may see your good works, and glorify your Fa-
ther who is in heaven. 17 Do not think that I am come to destroy the law, or the prophets. I am not
come to destroy, but to fulfill. 18 For amen I say unto you, till heaven and earth pass, one jot, or one
tittle shall not pass of the law, till all be fulfilled. 19 He therefore that shall break one of these least
commandments, and shall so teach men, shall be called the least in the kingdom of heaven. But he
that shall do and teach, he shall be called great in the kingdom of heaven. 20 For I tell you, that unless
your justice abound more than that of the scribes and Pharisees, you shall not enter into the kingdom
of heaven.

21 You have heard that it was said to them of old: Thou shalt not kill. And whosoever shall kill
shall be in danger of the judgment. 22 But I say to you, that whosoever is angry with his brother, shall
be in danger of the judgment. And whosoever shall say to his brother, Raca, shall be in danger of the
council. And whosoever shall say, Thou Fool, shall be in danger of hell fire. 23 If therefore thou offer
thy gift at the altar, and there thou remember that thy brother hath any thing against thee; 24 Leave
there thy offering before the altar, and go first to be reconciled to thy brother: and then coming thou
shalt offer thy gift. 25 Be at agreement with thy adversary betimes, whilst thou art in the way with
him: lest perhaps the adversary deliver thee to the judge, and the judge deliver thee to the officer, and
thou be cast into prison.

26 Amen I say to thee, thou shalt not go out from thence till thou repay the last farthing. 27 You
have heard that it was said to them of old: Thou shalt not commit adultery. 28 But I say to you, that
whosoever shall look on a woman to lust after her, hath already committed adultery with her in his

heart. 29 And if thy right eye scandalize thee, pluck it out and cast it from thee. For it is expedient for thee that one of thy members should perish, rather than that thy whole body be cast into hell. 30 And if thy right hand scandalize thee, cut it off, and cast it from thee: for it is expedient for thee that one of thy members should perish, rather than that thy whole body be cast into hell.

31 And it hath been said, whosoever shall put away his wife, let him give her a bill of divorce. 32 But I say to you, that whosoever shall put away his wife, excepting for the cause of fornication, maketh her to commit adultery: and he that shall marry her that is put away, committeth adultery. 33 Again you have heard that it was said to them of old, Thou shalt not forswear thyself: but thou shalt perform thy oaths to the Lord. 34 But I say to you not to swear at all, neither by heaven, for it is the throne of God: 35 Nor by the earth, for it is his footstool: nor by Jerusalem, for it is the city of the great king:

36 Neither shalt thou swear by thy head, because thou canst not make one hair white or black. 37 But let your speech be yea, yea: no, no: and that which is over and above these, is of evil. 38 You have heard that it hath been said, An eye for an eye, and a tooth for a tooth. 39 But I say to you not to resist evil: but if one strike thee on thy right cheek, turn to him also the other: 40 And if a man will contend with thee in judgment, and take away thy coat, let go thy cloak also unto him.

41 And whosoever will force thee one mile, go with him other two, 42 Give to him that asketh of thee and from him that would borrow of thee turn not away. 43 You have heard that it hath been said, Thou shalt love thy neighbor, and hate thy enemy. 44 But I say to you, Love your enemies: do good to them that hate you: and pray for them that persecute and calumniate you: 45 That you may be the children of your Father who is in heaven, who maketh his sun to rise upon the good, and bad, and raineth upon the just and the unjust.

46 For if you love them that love you, what reward shall you have? do not even the publicans this? 47 And if you salute your brethren only, what do you more? do not also the heathens this? 48 Be you therefore perfect, as also your heavenly Father is perfect.[23]

Outline

Construct an outline for an essay on the following question. What were the most significant events in the public ministry, passion, death, and resurrection of Jesus?

23 *Douay-Rheims Bible,* website. Edited by Richard Challoner. Drbo.org. http://www.drbo.org/chapter/47005.htm. Accessed April 20, 2021.

Lesson 24

The Apostolic Age

Vocabulary

Define each term in 5 sentences.

Pentecost

Twelve Apostles

St. Paul

Quiz

From the Lecture

1. Who was the first Christian martyr?
   A. St. Peter
   B. St. James
   C. St. Stephen
   D. St. Paul

2. Who was the first Gentile convert to Christianity?
   A. Saul
   B. Gaius
   C. Agrippa
   D. Cornelius

3. What was the resolution of the Council of Jerusalem?
   A. Jesus is fully God and man.
   B. Gentile converts do not have to follow the Mosaic Law.
   C. Mary is the mother of God.
   D. The Bible is the main authority for Church teachings.

4. What emperor led the persecution in which St. Peter and St. Paul were martyred?
   - A. Claudius
   - B. Diocletian
   - C. Nero
   - D. Tiberius

5. St. Peter was beheaded in Rome.
   - A. True
   - B. False

From the Textbook

6. Who was chosen as the replacement of Judas?
   - A. St. Paul
   - B. St. Jude
   - C. St. Stephen
   - D. St. Matthias

7. In Antioch, what was the new label given to members of the faith based on the teachings of Jesus?
   - A. Catholics
   - B. Christians
   - C. Nazoreans
   - D. Jesuits

8. Where was St. Thomas sent with the dispersal of the apostles?
   - A. India
   - B. Iran
   - C. Italy
   - D. Spain

9. Why did St. Paul go to Rome?
   - A. to meet Peter
   - B. to "appeal to Caesar"
   - C. to become pope
   - D. to be crucified

10. What group was responsible for leading the Jewish revolt against Rome in AD 66?
   - A. Christians
   - B. Hellenized Jews
   - C. followers of Herod
   - D. Zealots

Writing Assignment

Read the following excerpt from the Acts of the Apostles. Write a short 300-word essay answering the following question. What changed with the apostles on Pentecost?

Acts of the Apostles, 2:1–15, 38–47

1 And when the days of the Pentecost were accomplished, they were all together in one place: 2
And suddenly there came a sound from heaven, as of a mighty wind coming, and it filled the whole
house where they were sitting. 3 And there appeared to them parted tongues as it were of fire, and it
sat upon every one of them: 4 And they were all filled with the Holy Ghost, and they began to speak
with divers tongues, according as the Holy Ghost gave them to speak. 5 Now there were dwelling at
Jerusalem, Jews, devout men, out of every nation under heaven.

6 And when this was noised abroad, the multitude came together, and were confounded in mind,
because that every man heard them speak in his own tongue. 7 And they were all amazed, and won-
dered, saying: Behold, are not all these, that speak, Galileans? 8 And how have we heard, every man
our own tongue wherein we were born? 9 Parthians, and Medes, and Elamites, and inhabitants of
Mesopotamia, Judea, and Cappadocia, Pontus and Asia, 10 Phrygia, and Pamphylia, Egypt, and the
parts of Libya about Cyrene, and strangers of Rome,

11 Jews also, and proselytes, Cretes, and Arabians: we have heard them speak in our own tongues
the wonderful works of God. 12 And they were all astonished, and wondered, saying one to another:
What meaneth this? 13 But others mocking, said: These men are full of new wine. 14 But Peter stand-
ing up with the eleven, lifted up his voice, and spoke to them: Ye men of Judea, and all you that dwell
in Jerusalem, be this known to you, and with your ears receive my words. 15 For these are not drunk,
as you suppose, seeing it is but the third hour of the day:

38 But Peter said to them: Do penance, and be baptized every one of you in the name of Jesus
Christ, for the remission of your sins: and you shall receive the gift of the Holy Ghost. 39 For the
promise is to you, and to your children, and to all that are far off, whomsoever the Lord our God shall
call. 40 And with very many other words did he testify and exhort them, saying: Save yourselves from
this perverse generation...

41 They therefore that received his word, were baptized; and there were added in that day about
three thousand souls. 42 And they were persevering in the doctrine of the apostles, and in the com-
munication of the breaking of bread, and in prayers. 43 And fear came upon every soul: many won-
ders also and signs were done by the apostles in Jerusalem, and there was great fear in all. 44 And all
they that believed, were together, and had all things common. 45 Their possessions and goods they
sold, and divided them to all, according as every one had need.

46 And continuing daily with one accord in the temple, and breaking bread from house to house,
they took their meat with gladness and simplicity of heart; 47 Praising God, and having favour with
all the people. And the Lord increased daily together such as should be saved.[24]

24 *Douay-Rheims Bible*, website. Edited by Richard Challoner. Drbo.org. http://www.drbo.org/chapter/51002.htm. Accessed May 19, 2021.

Outline

Construct an outline for an essay on the following questions. What was the role of the apostles and St. Paul in the establishment of the Church? What controversies and challenges did they face?

Lesson 25

The Culture of the Early Church

Vocabulary

Define each term in 5 sentences.

Church Buildings

Christian Calendar and Rituals

Early Church Clergy and Members

Quiz

From the Lecture

1. When was the list of New Testament books formally accepted by the Church?
   - A. during the life Jesus
   - B. in the first century by the apostles
   - C. Church councils in the fourth century
   - D. Council of Trent

2. Where did most Christians worship for the first three centuries of the Church?
   - A. homes
   - B. churches
   - C. catacombs
   - D. temples

3. In Rome, what was the original name of churches associated with house churches?
   - A. basilicas
   - B. titular churches
   - C. cathedrals
   - D. catacombs

4. What are the first two letters of "Christ" in Greek?
    A. Chi Rho
    B. Alpha Omega
    C. Pi Tau
    D. Delta Alpha

5. What best describes the Alexamenos Graffito?
    A. a representation of Jesus as the Alpha and Omega
    B. the Good Shepard
    C. a sacrilegious mockery of an early Christian
    D. the Lamb of God

6. What did Constantine use as a model for Christian churches?
    A. temples
    B. baths
    C. domus
    D. basilicas

7. What is the root of the word "Cathedral"?
    A. church
    B. bishop
    C. chair
    D. large

8. The Roman (Julian) calendar is a lunar calendar.
    A. True
    B. False

9. What is the origin of the diocese?
    A. Constantine developed it for Church leaders.
    B. Jews in the diaspora used it for their rabbis.
    C. Celts used it to organize their tribes.
    D. Romans created it to divide provinces.

10. What is the Greek root of the word for "pope"?
    A. father
    B. brother
    C. chief
    D. priest

Writing Assignment

Read the following excerpt from the *Didache*. Write a short 300-word essay answering the following question. What were the rituals, prayers, and organization of early Christianity?

Chapter VIII

1 Let not your fasts be with the hypocrites, for they fast on Mondays and Thursdays, but do you fast on Wednesdays and Fridays. 2 And do not pray as the hypocrites, but as the Lord commanded in his Gospel, pray thus: "Our Father, who art in Heaven, hallowed be thy Name, thy Kingdom come, thy will be done, as in Heaven so also upon earth; give us to-day our daily bread, and forgive us our debt as we forgive our debtors, and lead us not into trial, but deliver us from the Evil One, for thine is the power and the glory for ever." 3 Pray thus three times a day.

Chapter IX

1 And concerning the Eucharist, hold Eucharist thus: 2 First concerning the Cup, "We give thanks to thee, our Father, for the Holy Vine of David thy child, which, thou didst make known to us through Jesus thy child; to thee be glory for ever." 3 And concerning the broken Bread: "We give thee thanks, our Father, for the life and knowledge which thou didst make known to us through Jesus thy Child. To thee be glory for ever. 4 As this broken bread was scattered upon the mountains, but was brought together and became one, so let thy Church be gathered together from the ends of the earth into thy Kingdom, for thine is the glory and the power through Jesus Christ for ever." 5 But let none eat or drink of your Eucharist except those who have been baptised in the Lord's Name. For concerning this also did the Lord say, "Give not that which is holy to the dogs."

Chapter X

1 But after you are satisfied with food, thus give thanks: 2 "We give thanks to thee, O Holy Father, for thy Holy Name which thou didst make to tabernacle in our hearts, and for the knowledge and faith and immortality which thou didst make known to us through Jesus thy Child. To thee be glory for ever. 3 Thou, Lord Almighty, didst create all things for thy Name's sake, and didst give food and drink to men for their enjoyment, that they might give thanks to thee, but us hast thou blessed with spiritual food and drink and eternal light through thy Child. 4 Above all we give thanks to thee for that thou art mighty. To thee be glory for ever. 5 Remember, Lord, thy Church, to deliver it from all evil and to make it perfect in thy love, and gather it together in its holiness from the four winds to thy kingdom which thou hast prepared for it. For thine is the power and the glory for ever. 6 Let grace come and let this world pass away. Hosannah to the God of David. If any man be holy, let him come! if any man be not, let him repent: Maranatha, Amen." 7 But suffer the prophets to hold Eucharist as they will.

Chapter XIV

1 On the Lord's Day of the Lord come together, break bread and hold Eucharist, after confessing your transgressions that your offering may be pure; 2 but let none who has a quarrel with his fellow join in your meeting until they be reconciled, that your sacrifice be not defiled. 3 For this is that which was spoken by the Lord, "In every place and time offer me a pure sacrifice, for I am a great king," saith the Lord, "and my name is wonderful among the heathen."

Chapter XV

1 Appoint therefore for yourselves bishops and deacons worthy of the Lord, meek men, and not lovers of money, and truthful and approved, for they also minister to you the ministry of the prophets and teachers. 2 Therefore do not despise them, for they are your honorable men together with the prophets and teachers. 3 And reprove one another not in wrath but in peace as you find in the Gospel, and let none speak with any who has done a wrong to his neighbor, nor let him hear a word from you until he repents. 4 But your prayers and alms and all your acts perform as ye find in the Gospel of our Lord.[25]

Outline

Construct an outline for an essay on the following question. What was the culture of the early Church, including building, calendars, and organization?

25 *Didache, ebook.* Translated by Kirsopp Lake. Wikisource. https://en.wikisource.org/wiki/Didache_(Lake_translation). Accessed May 31, 2021.

Lesson 26

The Roman Empire

Vocabulary

Define each term in 5 sentences.

Julio-Claudian Dynasty

The Good Emperors

The Terrible Third Century

Quiz

From the Lecture

1. Who followed Augustus as emperor of Rome?
   - A. Nero
   - B. Claudius
   - C. Tiberius
   - D. Caligula

2. What area was added to the Roman Empire under the rule of Claudius?
   - A. Spain
   - B. Egypt
   - C. Palestine
   - D. Britain

3. The Julio-Claudian Dynasty comes to an end after the death of Nero?
   - A. True
   - B. False

4. What was built by the Flavian emperors?
    A. the Golden House
    B. the Pantheon
    C. the Baths of Caracalla
    D. the Colosseum

5. Who was not one of the five "Good Emperors"?
    A. Trajan
    B. Hadrian
    C. Antoninus Pius
    D. Septimius

6. What is true about Marcus Aurelius?
    A. He was a philosopher.
    B. He had a peaceful reign.
    C. He fought as a gladiator.
    D. He was the first of the "Good Emperors."

7. What was the population of Rome during the height of the Roman Empire?
    A. 500,000
    B. 1,500,000
    C. 5,000,000
    D. 10,000,000

8. What power overthrew the Parthian Empire?
    A. Romans
    B. Greeks
    C. Sassanids
    D. Egyptians

9. Gladiators mainly fought in the Circus Maximus.
    A. True
    B. False

10. What best describes the emperors of the third century?
    A. good emperors
    B. long reigns
    C. Christian sympathizers
    D. killed after a short reign

Writing Assignment

Read the following excerpt from the *Historia Augusta*. Write a short 300-word essay answering the following question. How did the life of Commodus demonstrate the moral decline of Rome?

Historia Augusta

He engaged in gladiatorial combats, and accepted the names usually given to gladiators with as much pleasure as if he had been granted triumphal decorations. He regularly took part in the spectacles, and as often as he did so, ordered the fact to be inscribed in the public records. It is said that he engaged in gladiatorial bouts seven hundred and thirty-five times.

Besides these facts, it is related in records that he fought 365 gladiatorial combats in his father's reign. Afterwards, by vanquishing or slaying retiarii, he won enough gladiatorial crowns to bring the number up to a thousand. He also killed with his own hand thousands of wild beasts of all kinds, even elephants. And he frequently did these things before the eyes of the Roman people.

Such was his prowess in the slaying of wild beasts, that he once transfixed an elephant with a pole, pierced a gazelle's horn with a spear, and on a thousand occasions dispatched a mighty beast with a single blow. Such was his complete indifference to propriety, that time and again he sat in the theatre or amphitheatre dressed in a woman's garments and drank quite publicly.

Commodus himself was so lazy and careless in signing documents that he answered many petitions with the same formula, while in very many letters he merely wrote the word "Farewell". All official business was carried on by others, who, it is said, even used condemnations to swell their purses. And because he was so careless, moreover, a great famine arose in Rome, not because there was any real shortage of crops, but merely because those who then ruled the state were plundering the food supply. As for those who plundered on every hand, Commodus afterwards put them to death and confiscated their property; but for the time he pretended that a golden age had come, "Commodian" by name, and ordered a general reduction of prices, the result of which was an even greater scarcity.

In his reign many a man secured punishment for another or immunity for himself by bribery. Indeed, in return for money Commodus would grant a change of punishment, the right of burial, the alleviation of wrongs, and the substitution of another for one condemned to be put to death. He sold provinces and administrative posts, part of the proceeds accruing to those through whom he made the sale and part to Commodus himself. To some he sold even the lives of their enemies. Under him the imperial freedmen sold even the results of law-suits. He did not long put up with Paternus and Perennis as prefects; indeed, not one of the prefects whom he himself had appointed remained in office as long as three years. Most of them he killed, some with poison, some with the sword. Prefects of the city he changed with equal readiness. He executed his chamberlains with no compunctions whatever, even though all that he had done had been at their bidding. One of these chamberlains, however, Eclectus by name, forestalled him when he saw how ready Commodus was to put the chamberlains to death, and took part in a conspiracy to kill him.

At gladiatorial shows he would come to watch and stay to fight, covering his bare shoulders with a purple cloth. And it was his custom, moreover, to order the insertion in the city-gazette of everything he did that was base or foul or cruel, or typical of a gladiator or a procurer — at least, the writings of Marius Maximus so testify. He entitled the Roman people the "People of Commodus," since he had very often fought as a gladiator in their presence. And although the people regularly applauded him in his frequent combats as though he were a god, he became convinced that he was being laughed at, and gave orders that the Roman people should be slain in the Amphitheatre by the marines who spread the awnings. He gave an order, also, for the burning of the city, as though it were his private colony, and this order would have been executed had not Laetus, the prefect of the guard, deterred him. Among other triumphal titles, he was also given the name "Captain of the Secutores" six hundred and twenty times.

Because of these things — but all too late — Quintus Aemilius Laetus, prefect of the guard, and Marcia, his concubine, were roused to action and entered into a conspiracy against his life. First they gave him poison; and when this proved ineffective they had him strangled by the athlete with whom he was accustomed to exercise.

The people and senate demanded that his body be dragged with the hook and cast into the Tiber; later, however, at the bidding of Pertinax, it was borne to the Mausoleum of Hadrian.[26]

Outline

Construct an outline for an essay on the following questions. Who were some of the important Roman emperors? What were their successes and failures?

26 *Historia Augusta, ebook.* Translated by David Magie. LacusCurtius. https://penelope.uchicago.edu/Thayer/e/roman/texts/historia_augusta/commodus*.html. Accessed May 23, 2021.

Lesson 27

Early Popes and Martyrs

Vocabulary

Define each term in 5 sentences.

Christian tension with Rome

Early Heresies

Early Church Fathers and Popes

Quiz

From the Lecture

1. St. Clement I was the fourth pope.
    - A. True
    - B. False

2. What was the role of St. Apollonius before his martyrdom?
    - A. farmer
    - B. slave
    - C. soldier
    - D. senator

3. What was the Jewish-Christian group that accepted some Christian principles but clung to the Jewish law?
    - A. Gnostics
    - B. Ebionites
    - C. Modalists
    - D. Zealots

4. What was promised to members of Gnosticism?
   A. hidden knowledge
   B. immortality
   C. power and wealth
   D. healing powers

5. Who among the Apostolic Fathers was a follower of St. John, the apostle?
   A. St. Justin
   B. St. Augustine
   C. St. Polycarp
   D. St. Irenaeus

6. St. Clement wrote a letter to a church is what city?
   A. Athens
   B. Rome
   C. Alexandria
   D. Corinth

7. What movement was associated with Cerinthus?
   A. Zealots
   B. Arians
   C. Gnosticism
   D. Judaism

8. St. Polycarp tried to convince the Romans to celebrate Easter on Sunday.
   A. True
   B. False

9. Montanus preached an imminent end of the world and that the faithful should gather in a New Jerusalem in:
   A. Rome.
   B. Antioch.
   C. Byzantium.
   D. Pepuza.

10. Who was the antipope who denied absolution for numerous unforgivable sins but later reconciled with the Church when exiled to the mines?
   A. Origen
   B. Hippolytus
   C. Cletus
   D. Ignatius

Writing Assignment

Read the following excerpt from the *First Epistle of Clement*. Write a short 300-word essay answering the following questions. How were clerical roles passed down in the early Church? As pope, how did Clement assert his authority?

1 Clement 42

1. The Apostles received the Gospel for us from the Lord Jesus Christ; Jesus Christ was sent forth from God. 2. So then Christ is from God, and the Apostles are from Christ. Both therefore came of the will of God in the appointed order. 3. Having therefore received a charge, and having been fully assured through the resurrection of our Lord Jesus Christ and confirmed in the word of God with full assurance of the Holy Ghost, they went forth with the glad tidings that the kingdom of God should come. 4. So preaching everywhere in country and town, they appointed their firstfruits, when they had proved them by the Spirit, to be bishops and deacons unto them that should believe. 5. And this they did in no new fashion; for indeed it had been written concerning bishops and deacons from very ancient times; for thus saith the scripture in a certain place, I will appoint their bishops in righteousness and their deacons in faith.

1 Clement 44

1. And our Apostles knew through our Lord Jesus Christ that there would be strife over the name of the bishop's office. 2. For this cause therefore, having received complete foreknowledge, they appointed the aforesaid persons, and afterwards they provided a continuance, that if these should fall asleep, other approved men should succeed to their ministration. Those therefore who were appointed by them, or afterward by other men of repute with the consent of the whole Church, and have ministered unblamably to the flock of Christ in lowliness of mind, peacefully and with all modesty, and for long time have borne a good report with all these men we consider to be unjustly thrust out from their ministration. 3. For it will be no light sin for us, if we thrust out those who have offered the gifts of the bishop's office unblamably and holily. 4. Blessed are those presbyters who have gone before, seeing that their departure was fruitful and ripe: for they have no fear lest any one should remove them from their appointed place. 5. For we see that ye have displaced certain persons, though they were living honorably, from the ministration which had been respected by them blamelessly.

1 Clement 58

1. Let us therefore be obedient unto His most holy and glorious Name, thereby escaping the threatenings which were spoken of old by the mouth of Wisdom against them which disobey, that we may dwell safely, trusting in the most holy Name of His majesty. 2. Receive our counsel, and ye shall have no occasion of regret. For as God liveth, and the Lord Jesus Christ liveth, and the Holy Spirit, who are the faith and the hope of the elect, so surely shall he, who with lowliness of mind and instant in gentleness hath without regretfulness performed the ordinances and commandments that are given by God, be enrolled and have a name among the number of them that are saved through Jesus Christ, through whom is the glory unto Him for ever and ever. Amen.

1 Clement 59

1. But if certain persons should be disobedient unto the words spoken by Him through us, let them understand that they will entangle themselves in no slight transgression and danger; 2. but we shall be guiltless of this sin. And we will ask, with instancy of prayer and supplication, that the Creator of the universe may guard intact unto the end the number that hath been numbered of His elect throughout the whole world, through His beloved Son Jesus Christ, through whom He called us from darkness to light, from ignorance to the full knowledge of the glory of His Name. 3. [Grant unto us, Lord,] that we may set our hope on Thy Name which is the primal source of all creation, and open the eyes of our hearts, that we may know Thee, who alone abidest Highest in the lofty, Holy in the holy; who layest low in the insolence of the proud, who settest the lowly on high, and bringest the lofty low; who makest rich and makest poor; who killest and makest alive; who alone art the Benefactor of spirits and the God of all flesh; who lookest into the abysses, who scanest the works of man; the Succor of them that are in peril, the Savior of them that are in despair; The Creator and Overseer of every spirit; who multipliest the nations upon earth, and hast chosen out from all men those that love Thee through Jesus Christ, Thy beloved Son, through whom Thou didst instruct us, didst sanctify us, didst honor us. 4. We beseech Thee, Lord and Master, to be our help and succor. Save those among us who are in tribulation; have mercy on the lowly; lift up the fallen; show Thyself unto the needy; heal the ungodly; convert the wanderers of Thy people; feed the hungry; release our prisoners; raise up the weak; comfort the fainthearted. Let all the Gentiles know that Thou art the God alone, and Jesus Christ is Thy Son, and we are Thy people and the sheep of Thy pasture.[27]

Outline

Construct an outline for an essay on the following questions. What were the persecutions and heresies that challenged the early Church? How did the early popes and Church Fathers respond?

27 Clement. *First Epistle of Clement.* Translated by Joseph Barber. Wikisource. Lightfoot. https://en.wikisource.org/wiki/1_Clement_(Lightfoot_translation). Accessed May 20, 2021.

Lesson 28

The Great Persecution

Vocabulary

Define each term in 5 sentences.

Tetrarch

Diocletian

Persecution under Diocletian and Galerius

Quiz

From the Lecture

1. What was the main point of contention between Antipope Novatian and Pope Cornelius?
    - A. the nature of Jesus
    - B. the role of the Holy Spirit
    - C. penance for apostates
    - D. the role of the pope

2. How was St. Lawrence killed?
    - A. grilled
    - B. beheaded
    - C. crucified
    - D. eaten by wild beasts

3. What does "homoousios" mean?
    - A. our father
    - B. consubstantial
    - C. emperor
    - D. god

4. How many members did the imperial college have in the tetrarch?
    - A. 2
    - B. 3
    - C. 4
    - D. 9

5. Who proclaimed Constantine emperor?
    - A. Galerius
    - B. Diocletian
    - C. the senate
    - D. the army

From the Textbook

6. Who issued an edict of persecution in 250 against Christians?
    - A. Diocletian
    - B. Nero
    - C. Decius
    - D. Claudius

7. Why was St. Tarcisius beaten to death?
    - A. He hid the Blessed Sacrament.
    - B. He refused to offer a sacrifice to the Roman gods.
    - C. He was revealed as Christian by his rivals.
    - D. He spoke publicly against the edict of the emperor.

8. How did the emperor Valerian die?
    - A. killed by his soldiers
    - B. of old age
    - C. as prisoner of the king of Persia
    - D. in the Colosseum

9. What did the emperor Aurelian build in Rome?
    - A. colosseum
    - B. palace
    - C. temple to June
    - D. walls

10. In the tetrarchy, who did Diocletian pick to be Caesar in the west?
    - A. Galerius
    - B. Maximian
    - C. Constantius
    - D. Decius

Writing Assignment

Read the following excerpt from Eusebius of Caesarea's *The History of the Martyrs in Palestine*. Write a short 300-word essay answering the following question. How did the martyrs react to the threat of death?

The History of the Martyrs in Palestine

THE CONFESSION OF ALPHAEUS, AND ZACCHAEUS, AND ROMANUS, IN THE FIRST YEAR OF THE PERSECUTION IN OUR DAYS.

IT happened, at the same time, that the festival, which is celebrated on the twentieth year of the emperor's reign, was at hand, and a pardon was announced at that festival for the offences of those who were in prison. The governor, therefore, of the country came before the festival, and instituted an inquiry respecting the prisoners which were in confinement, and some of them were set at liberty through the clemency of the emperors; but the martyrs of God he insulted with tortures, as though they were worse malefactors than thieves and murderers.

Zacchaeus, therefore, who had been a deacon of the Church in the city of Gadara, was led like an innocent lamb from the flock—for such indeed he was by nature, and those of his acquaintance had given him the appellation of Zacchaeus as a mark of honour, calling him by the name of that first Zacchaeus—for one reason, because of the smallness of his stature, and for another, on account of the strict life which he led; and he was even more desirous of seeing our Lord than the first Zacchaeus. And when he was brought in before the judge, he rejoiced in his confession for the sake of Christ: and when he had spoken the words of God before the judge, he was delivered over to all the tortures of punishment, and after having been first scourged, he was made to endure dreadful lacerations, and then after this he was thrown into prison again, and there for a whole day and a whole night his feet were strained to four holes of the rack. . . .

And on this same day also Romanus suffered martyrdom in the city of Antioch. But this Romanus belonged to Palestine, and he was a Deacon, and an Exorcist likewise, in one of the villages of Caesarea. And he, too, was stretched out upon the rack, and like as the martyr Alphaeus had done in Caesarea, so did the blessed Romanus by his words of denunciation restrain from sacrificing those who, from their timidity, were relapsed into the sin of the error of devils, recalling to the minds of them all the terrors of God. He had also the courage to go in together with the; multitude who were dragged by force into error and to present himself there in Antioch before the judge: and when he heard the judge commanding them to sacrifice, and they, in trepidation from their fears, were driven with trembling to offer sacrifice, this zealous man was no longer able to endure this sad spectacle, but was : moved with pity towards them as towards those who were feeling about in thick darkness, and on the point of falling over a precipice, and so he made the doctrine of the religion of God to rise up before them like the sun, crying aloud and saying: Whither are ye being carried, oh men? Are ye all stooping down to cast yourselves into the abyss? Lift up the eyes of your understanding on high, and above all the worlds ye shall recognize God and the Savior of all the ends of the world; and do not abandon for error the commandment which has been committed to you: then shall the godless error of the worship of devils be apparent to you. Remember also the righteous judgment of God supreme, And when he had spoken these things to them with a loud voice, and stood there without fear and without dread, at the command of him who was constituted judge there, the officers seized him, and he condemned him to be destroyed by fire, for the crafty judge perceived that many were confirmed by the words which the martyr spoke, and that he turned many back from error. And because the servant of Jesus had done these things in the place where the emperors were, they at once brought out this blessed man into the midst of the city of Antioch. And he was arrived at the spot where he was to undergo his punishment, and the things which were required for the fire were got ready, and they were busying themselves to fulfil the command with haste, when the emperor Diocletian, having heard of what was done, gave orders that they should withdraw the martyr from the death by fire, because, said he, his insolence and folly were not suitable for punishment by fire; and so, like a merciful emperor, he gave order for a new kind of punishment for the martyr, that his tongue should be cut out. Nevertheless, when that member by which he spoke was taken away, still was his true love not severed from his God; neither was his intellectual tongue restrained from preaching, and immediately he received from God, the sovereign of all, a recompense for his struggle in the conflict, and was filled with power much greater than he had before. Then did great wonder seize upon all men; for he, whose tongue had been cut out, forthwith, by the gift of God spoke out valiantly, and heartily exulted in the faith, as though he were standing by the side of Him in whom he made his confession; and with a countenance bright and cheerful he saluted his acquaintance, and scattered the seed of the word of God into the ears of all men, exhorting them all to worship God alone, and lifting up his prayers and thanksgiving to God, who worketh marvels: and when he had done these things he mightily gave testimony to the word of Christ before all men, and in deed shewed forth the power of Him in whom he made his confession. And when he had done so for a long time he was again stretched upon the rack; and by the command of the governor and the judge they threw upon him the strangling instrument, and he was strangled. And on the same day as those blessed martyrs who appertained to Zacchaeus he was consummated in his confession. And although this man actually passed through the conflict, and suffered martyrdom in Antioch, nevertheless, because his family was of Palestine, he is properly described among the company of martyrs in this our country.[28]

Outline

Construct an outline for an essay on the following questions. What were the problems facing the Roman Empire at the end of the third century and the beginning of the fourth century? How did the emperors attack Christians during this time?

28 Eusebius of Caesarea. *The History of the Martyrs in Palestine, ebook.* Translated by William Cureton. The Tertullian Project. https://www.tertullian.org/fathers/eusebius_martyrs.htm. Accessed May 27, 2021.

Lesson 29

CONSTANTINE

Vocabulary

Define each term in 5 sentences.

Vision and Conversion of Constantine

Constantine's Christian Policies

Donatists and Arians

Quiz

From the Lecture

1. What was Helena's relationship to Constantine?
    - A. wife
    - B. mother
    - C. half-sister
    - D. daughter

2. According to Eusebius, what did Constantine see in the sky?
    - A. an army of angels
    - B. Jesus
    - C. a cross
    - D. a circle

3. The Edict of Milan made Christianity the official religion of Rome.
    - A. True
    - B. False

4. What belief best describes the Arians?
    A. German tribes are superior to Romans.
    B. An apostate Christian can return without doing penance.
    C. Christians must continue the practice of circumcision.
    D. Jesus is subordinate to the Father.

5. When was Constantine baptized?
    A. at birth
    B. after his vision
    C. at the Council of Nicaea
    D. at the end of his life

From the Textbook

6. Who married Constantine's sister to form an alliance?
    A. Daia
    B. Maxentius
    C. Galerius
    D. Licinius

7. Where did Constantine defeat Maxentius in 312?
    A. Rome
    B. Rhine River
    C. Milvian Bridge
    D. Appian Way

8. Where did Constantine and Licinius meet to form an alliance and agree on a tolerant policy towards Christians?
    A. Milan
    B. Rome
    C. Athens
    D. Nicomedia

9. Who was the leader and namesake of the rigorist faction towards repentant apostates?
    A. Arius
    B. Donatus
    C. Alexander
    D. Sylvester

10. What adjustment to the Roman calendar was initiated by Constantine?
    A. solar calendar
    B. Sunday as a day of rest
    C. Lent
    D. ember days

Writing Assignment

Read the following exerpts from Eusebius of Caesarea's *Life of Constantine*. Write a short 300-word essay answering the following question. How did Constantine convert from a pagan to a Christian?

Chapter XXVII.

That after reflecting on the Downfall of those who had worshiped Idols, he made Choice of Christianity.

Being convinced, however, that he needed some more powerful aid than his military forces could afford him, on account of the wicked and magical enchantments which were so diligently practiced by the tyrant, he sought Divine assistance, deeming the possession of arms and a numerous soldiery of secondary importance, but believing the co-operating power of Deity invincible and not to be shaken. He considered, therefore, on what God he might rely for protection and assistance. While engaged in this enquiry, the thought occurred to him, that, of the many emperors who had preceded him, those who had rested their hopes in a multitude of gods, and served them with sacrifices and offerings, had in the first place been deceived by flattering predictions, and oracles which promised them all prosperity, and at last had met with an unhappy end, while not one of their gods had stood by to warn them of the impending wrath of heaven; while one alone who had pursued an entirely opposite course, who had condemned their error, and honored the one Supreme God during his whole life, had found him to be the Savior and Protector of his empire, and the Giver of every good thing. Reflecting on this, and well weighing the fact that they who had trusted in many gods had also fallen by manifold forms of death, without leaving behind them either family or offspring, stock, name, or memorial among men: while the God of his father had given to him, on the other hand, manifestations of his power and very many tokens: and considering farther that those who had already taken arms against the tyrant, and had marched to the battle-field under the protection of a multitude of gods, had met with a dishonorable end (for one of them had shamefully retreated from the contest without a blow, and the other, being slain in the midst of his own troops, became, as it were, the mere sport of death); reviewing, I say, all these considerations, he judged it to be folly indeed to join in the idle worship of those who were no gods, and, after such convincing evidence, to err from the truth; and therefore felt it incumbent on him to honor his father's God alone.

Chapter XXVIII.

How, while he was praying, God sent him a Vision of a Cross of Light in the Heavens at Mid-day, with an Inscription admonishing him to conquer by that.

Accordingly, he called on him with earnest prayer and supplications that he would reveal to him who he was, and stretch forth his right hand to help him in his present difficulties. And while he was thus praying with fervent entreaty, a most marvelous sign appeared to him from heaven, the account of which it might have been hard to believe had it been related by any other person. But since the victorious emperor himself long afterwards declared it to the writer of this history, when he was honored with his acquaintance and society, and confirmed his statement by an oath, who could hesitate to accredit the relation, especially since the testimony of after-time has established its truth? He said that about noon, when the day was already beginning to decline, he saw with his own eyes the trophy of a cross of light in the heavens, above the sun, and bearing the inscription, Conquer by this. At this sight he himself was struck with amazement, and his whole army also, which followed him on this expedition, and witnessed the miracle.

Chapter XXIX.

How the Christ of God appeared to him in his Sleep, and commanded him to use in his Wars a Standard made in the Form of the Cross.

He said, moreover, that he doubted within himself what the import of this apparition could be. And while he continued to ponder and reason on its meaning, night suddenly came on; then in his sleep the Christ of God appeared to him with the same sign which he had seen in the heavens, and commanded him to make a likeness of that sign which he had seen in the heavens, and to use it as a safeguard in all engagements with his enemies.

Chapter XXX.

The Making of the Standard of the Cross.

At dawn of day he arose, and communicated the marvel to his friends: and then, calling together the workers in gold and precious stones, he sat in the midst of them, and described to them the figure of the sign he had seen, bidding them represent it in gold and precious stones. And this representation I myself have had an opportunity of seeing.

Chapter XXXI.

A Description of the Standard of the Cross, which the Romans now call the Labarum.

Now it was made in the following manner. A long spear, overlaid with gold, formed the figure of the cross by means of a transverse bar laid over it. On the top of the whole was fixed a wreath of gold and precious stones; and within this, the symbol of the Saviour's name, two letters indicating the name of Christ by means of its initial characters, the letter P being intersected by X in its centre: and these letters the emperor was in the habit of wearing on his helmet at a later period. From the cross-bar of the spear was suspended a cloth, a royal piece, covered with a profuse embroidery of most brilliant precious stones; and which, being also richly interlaced with gold, presented an indescribable degree of beauty to the beholder. This banner was of a square form, and the upright staff, whose lower section was of great length, bore a golden half-length portrait of the pious emperor and his children on its upper part, beneath the trophy of the cross, and immediately above the embroidered banner.

The emperor constantly made use of this sign of salvation as a safeguard against every adverse and hostile power, and commanded that others similar to it should be carried at the head of all his armies.[29]

---

29 Eusebius of Caesarea. *Life of Constantine, ebook.* Translated by Philip Schaff. Wikisource. https://en.wikisource.org/wiki/Nicene_and_Post-Nicene_Fathers:_Series_II/Volume_I/Constantine/The_Life_of_Constantine/Book_I. Accessed on May 31, 2021.

Outline

Construct an outline for an essay on the following questions. How did Constantine convert to Christianity? What impact did he have on Christianity?

Lesson 30

The Final

Study Guide

Identifications (100 points)

State what/who, when, where, and significance of the following terms in five sentences for each term. Eight terms will be presented to you on the exam, and you will have to do five. Use the vocabulary assignments to help study.

1. Roman Conquest of Italy
2. Roman Legions
3. Punic War
4. Kings of Rome
5. Magistrates of Rome
6. Patricians and Plebians
7. Optimates and Populares
8. Soldier-Heroes (Marius, Sulla, Pompey)
9. Julius Caesar
10. Roman Heroes
11. Roman Families
12. Roman Religion
13. Second Triumvirate
14. Octavian's Triumph over Antony
15. Augustus' Political Settlement
16. Roman Buildings
17. Roman Trade
18. Roman Slavery
19. The Gospels
20. Herodian Rulers
21. The Holy Family
22. Public Ministry of Jesus
23. Passion and Death of Jesus
24. Jesus: Resurrection to Ascension

25. Pentecost
26. Twelve Apostles
27. St. Paul
28. Church Buildings
29. Christian Calendar and Rituals
30. Early Church Clergy and Members
31. Julio-Claudian Dynasty
32. The Good Emperors
33. The Terrible Third Century
34. Christian tension with Rome
35. Early Heresies
36. Early Church Fathers and Popes
37. Tetrarch
38. Diocletian
39. Persecution of Diocletian and Galerius
40. Vision and Conversion of Constantine
41. Constantine's Christian Policies
42. Donatist and Arians

Essays (100 Points)

In several short paragraphs, answer the following questions. Four questions will be presented to you, and you will have to do two. Use the outline assignments to help study.

1. How did Rome conquer the Mediterranean world? Why was their military so successful?
2. How did Rome transition from a kingdom to a republic? What were the main political features of the Roman Republic?
3. What were the main divisions and hostilities during the civil wars at the end of the Roman Republic?
4. What were the key elements of Roman culture, including literature, history, families, and religion?
5. How did Augustus come to power? What political and military actions did he do when in power?
6. What were the key elements of Roman society, including buildings, slavery, and trade?
7. What are the historical sources for Jesus? What was the historical context (Jewish and Roman) at the time of his birth?
8. What were the most significant events in the public ministry, passion, death, and resurrection of Jesus?

9. What was the role of the apostles and St. Paul in the establishment of the Church? What controversies and challenges did they face?

10. What was the culture of the early Church, including building, calendars, and organization?

11. Who were some of the important Roman emperors? What were their successes and failures?

12. What were the persecutions and heresies that challenged the early Church? How did the popes and Church Fathers respond?

13. What were the problems facing the Roman Empire at the end of the third century and the beginning of the fourth century? How did the emperors attack Christians during this time?

14. How did Constantine convert to Christianity? What impact did he have on Christianity?

Final Exam

A parent should randomly select eight terms from the identification section and four questions from the essay section. As with the midterm, the selections should be balanced and from different lessons. A sample exam is below. Students should have a set time to complete the exam (two hours is suggested), and they should not have access to notes, the textbook, or the internet.

Sample Final

Identifications (100 points)

State what/who, when, where and significance of five and only five of the following terms in five sentences for each term.

1. Roman Conquest of Italy
2. Julius Caesar
3. Second Triumvirate
4. Roman Slavery
5. Passion and Death of Jesus
6. Early Church Clergy and Members
7. The Good Emperors
8. Constantine's Christian Policies

Essays (100 Points)

In several short paragraphs, answer two and only two of following questions. Each of the two essays should have an introduction, several body paragraphs, and a conclusion.

1. How did Rome transition from a kingdom to a republic? What were the main political features of the Roman Republic?

2. What are the historical sources for Jesus? What was the historical context (Jewish and Roman) at the time of his birth?

3. What was the role of the apostles and St. Paul in the establishment of the Church? What controversies and challenges did they face?

4. What were the problems facing the Roman Empire at the end of the third century and the beginning of the fourth century? How did the emperors attack the Christian population during this time?

Grading the Final

The exams are worth 200 points. Each of the five terms is worth 20 points for a total of 100 points and each of the two essays is worth 50 points for a total of 100 points. The exams are based on the vocabulary and outline assignments, and the completed vocabulary and outlines assignments should be used as a guide to grade to the exam.

Answer Key

Quiz 1: a, b, c, c, c, b, d, a (p. 9), c (p. 10), a (p. 12)
Quiz 2: b, b, a, c, b, a, b, d (p. 25), b (p. 26), d (p. 27)
Quiz 3: b, a, b, d, a, d, b, b, d (p. 31), a (p. 32)
Quiz 4: a, b, b, a, d, c, b, c (p. 42), a (p. 45), d (p. 46)
Quiz 5: d, c, d, b, b, c, b, a (p. 62), b (p. 65), a (p. 72)
Quiz 6: a, d, d, a, b, d (p. 82), a (p. 87), c (p. 89), a (p. 92), c (p. 93)
Quiz 7: c, b, a, c, d, a, d, c, a (p. 107), b (p. 108)
Quiz 8: b, b, a, c, d, a (p. 101), d (p. 104), b (p. 109), d (p. 113), d (p. 122)
Quiz 9: a, d, b, b, c, d (p. 130), a (p. 131), b (p. 150), a (p. 155), b (p. 157)
Quiz 10: d, a, b, c, d, a, b, a, b (p. 163), c (p. 164)
Quiz 11: d, c, c, a, b, c, b (p. 178), d (p. 179), a (p. 180), b (p. 183)
Quiz 12: b, a, c, c, d, a, c, a, b, c
Quiz 13: a, c, b, d, c, d (p. 194), c (p. 196), a (p. 199) b (pp. 202–3) c (p. 206)
Quiz 14: c, b, d, a, c, a, d, a, b, a
Quiz 16: b, c, b, a, c, d (p. 212), b (p. 213), b (pp. 220–21), d (p. 222), a (p. 233)
Quiz 17: b, c, d, a, a, d, a (p. 216) b (p. 217), c (p. 217), a (pp. 217–8)
Quiz 18: b, c, d, a, d, d (p. 252), b (p. 252), a (p. 256), c (p. 257), a (p. 263)
Quiz 19: d, b, b, c, a, c, b, b, a, c
Quiz 20: a, d, c, a, c, a (p. 270) a (pp. 274–75), b (p. 279), d (p. 279), c (p. 281)
Quiz 21: a, b, d, b, a, c, a, c, a, a
Quiz 22: d, c, a, b, c, b (p. 290), b (p. 293), c (p. 295), d (p. 301), b (p. 303)
Quiz 23: a, b, d, a, c, d (p. 321), c (p. 328), d (p. 359), b (p. 366), d (p. 375)
Quiz 24: c, d, b, c, b, d (p. 395), b (p. 401), a (p. 407), b (p. 422), d (p. 425)
Quiz 25: c, a, b, a, c, d, c, b, d, a
Quiz 26: c, d, a, d, d, a, b, c, b, d
Quiz 27: a, d, b, a, c, d (p. 450), c (p. 452), b (p. 460), d (p. 464), b (pp. 469, 474)
Quiz 28: c, a, b, c, d, c (p. 491), a (p. 498), c (p. 499), d (p. 500), c (p. 502)
Quiz 29: b, c, b, d, d, d (p. 526), c (p. 529), a (p. 531), b (p. 533), b (p. 541)